The Artful Chicken

Great Recipes & Splendid Objects
for the Passionate Collector

LINDA ARNAUD

ORIGINAL PHOTOGRAPHY
MICHEL ARNAUD

DESIGN & ART DIRECTION
JOEL AVIROM

PROJECT EDITOR
CAROLE LALLI

Stewart, Tabori & Chang
New York

FOOD STYLING: MARIANN SAUVION AND GRADY BEST

DESIGN ASSISTANTS: MEGHAN DAY HEALEY AND JASON SNYDER

PAGE I: *Black-and-white roosters in a naïf style sit on a richly colored ground framed with a foliage border. The hooked rug is from the McAdoo Company of Vermont, a family of artisans now in their third generation.*

PAGES II & III: *A quaint and quirky cock crafted by a contemporary American-Indian artist.*

PAGE V: *This hen is of modern design and unlikely was made with any symbolic reference implied. Nevertheless, it is a charming coincidence that as a lantern it not only reflects a lovely light but the chicken's association with spiritual enlightenment.*

PAGES VI & VII: *Similar in color and style to a type of nesting hens associated with manufacturers at Staffordshire, England, this piece clearly shows the representational conventions adhered to in creating these covered dishes.*

Text copyright © Linda Arnaud 2000
Original photographs copyright © Michel Arnaud 2000; additional credits appear on pages 166–169, which shall be considered an extension of this page.

Published in 2000 by
Stewart, Tabori & Chang
A division of Harry N. Abrams, Inc.
115 West 18th Street
New York, NY 10011

Library of Congress Cataloging-in-Publication Data
Arnaud, Linda.
    The artful chicken : great recipes and splendid objects for the passionate collector / Linda Arnaud ; original photography by Michel Arnaud
    p. cm.
    ISBN 1-58479-022-9
    1. Cookery (Chicken) I. Title.

    TX750.5.C45 A76 2000
    641.6'65—dc21   00-022965

The text of this book was composed in Goudy Village, captions were composed in Goudy Village Italic.

Edited by Marisa Bulzone

Graphic Production by Pamela Schechter

Printed in Italy by Mondadori Printing

10 9 8 7 6 5 4 3 2 1
First Printing

For my parents
Nelle and Hal Homan

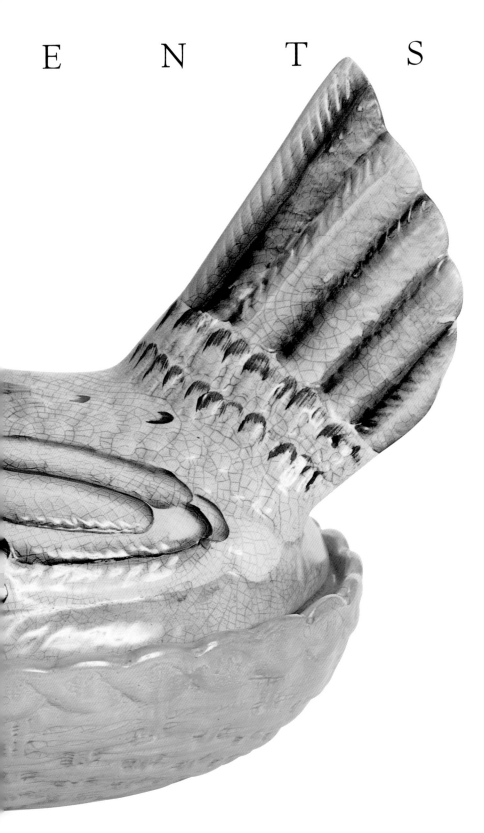

E N T S

Silver Spangles

Golden Pencilled Hamburghs

Silver Pencilled Hamburghs

S. Spangle
Mooney Cock

S. Pencilled
Henny Cock

Old Type Blacks

Gold Spangles

Modern Type Blacks. 1911

ACKNOWLEDGMENTS

I am indebted to many friends, relatives and new acquaintances who generously gave support and assistance in the making of this book. First among them are my husband Michel Arnaud and my great friend Joel Avirom; together they beautifully visualized my dream. I add grateful thanks to Carole Lalli for guidance throughout the project. Leslie Stoker and Marisa Bulzone at Stewart Tabori & Chang cheered us all on—their enthusiasm made this book possible.

Jason Snyder, Meghan Day Healey and Liana Fredley have my thanks for their diligent work in producing The Artful Chicken. Carla Lalli Music's assistance in the kitchen is much appreciated.

Private collectors, antique dealers, shop owners and others generously loaned treasured objects, along with interesting information about antiques or collectibles. Special thanks are offered to Sue Blair, Ron and Priscilla Richley, Ilene Bahr, Renato Danese, Robert Hicks, Richard Story and Jennifer Crandall, Joseph Mann, Joel Siegel and Ena Swansea, Patricia Carlisle and Melinda Hall, William Hicks, Sheila Klodney, Fernando Music, Danny Danoff of Bob Pryor Antiques, Howard Basis of Olde Antiques, Bill and Jane Heynes of William & Green, Carole Weiner and Barbara Bourgeois of Country Loft Antiques, Bonnie Mulville of April 56, Bob Rush of Church Street Trading Company, Carol Kappenhagen of Gracious Home, Elizabeth Leamon of Quimper Faience and McAdoo Rugs.

And a very special thank you to my family and friends who volunteered to taste the recipes before they were included in the book—and remained cheerful dinner companions on this steady diet of chicken.

INTRODUCTION

—🐓—

This book is about food and art.
I love to cook. I love to look. And I love to collect.

I AM EQUALLY HAPPY IN A FOOD MARKET, A GRAND museum, or a dusty antique shop.

And I am happiest of all at home around the dining table in the company of family and friends with a good home-cooked meal set out on a beautifully dressed table.

My first solo cooking experience was a simple Sunday breakfast prepared for my parents. Fried eggs. Hash from a can. Toast. And coffee. I was about ten. I remember that all the elements of the meal were well-timed and fairly properly cooked (though I did break a yolk). And why not—I had simply followed a sequence of preparation I had watched my mother execute for so many Sundays past.

I thought I had done something nice, not something remarkable. I also felt something nice: the same pride and pleasure my mother felt at each meal she prepared. I could tell because of the smile that crossed her face with the "Mom, this is great" that came after our first taste. I was hooked, and according to my mother, after that first breakfast I never looked back. The reward is that great.

This brass rooster card holder, marked with the slogan and name of a famous brewery, might have held a list of the beers at a typical brewers-owned pub in nineteenth century England. Today, it makes a handsome holder for a place card.

I had no fears and was certain that you could make any dish you wished if you followed a recipe from a cookbook. Armed with *The New York Times Cookbook* in my early teens and, later on, Julia Child's *Mastering the Art of French Cooking*, my culinary bible, a world of wonderful food opened up to me. From eggs and hash I went directly to Veal Sauté Marengo, Boeuf Bourguignon, Coq au Vin, and years of pleasure in the kitchen and at the table.

Long before genetics or conditioning were hot button issues, my family attributed my culinary bent to our heritage. My great-grandfather had been the equivalent of a grocer in the Ukraine. As a child, I had delighted in stories of how my grandmother and her sisters helped out at their father's store. They sometimes tossed cabbages and potatoes as a game and once had gotten slightly tipsy sampling—instead of just siphoning—liquor from shipping casks to bottles.

My grandfather and granduncles worked as dishwashers when they first arrived in America, then moved on to owning doughnut stands and shops selling very special doughnuts from their own recipe. A cafeteria or two and a restaurant followed in New York City.

Throughout my childhood I heard countless tales of family gatherings in New Jersey hosted by my grandaunt and her husband, who fed the clan on their own chickens and home-grown vegetables and fruits. My grandmother would bring her pirogis and noodles, which she had laid out to dry on special white linen cloths draped over every available surface in her home. These traditions continued, somewhat altered, into my childhood, and provide equally as pleasant memories of a convivial and bountiful table.

When I moved to England and then married a Frenchman, frequent travel and gatherings of family and friends focused even more emphatically on food. Business trips and family visits often meant a detour to or a stop at a celebrated restaurant in France or Italy and always included a traditional French family dinner. I soon became aware that culinary knowledge and expertise of the French kind is a birthright, and the education of the "uninitiated" a patriotic duty.

So my father-in-law, a wine representative by trade, taught me about cheese and wine at dinner and on excursions to vineyards, while my husband's godfather, Yves Auzolle, retired chef and owner of La Truite, a well-rated Paris restaurant in the fifties, refined my cooking. I knew I finally was "accepted" when I was complimented on my selection of a perfect Camembert, paired a Meursault correctly with a meal, and was asked to serve seconds of my rendition of the family's gratin Dauphinois.

Except for a few courses and lectures at a prestigious culinary school and with some chefs in England, my training for the kitchen has been truly informal, while my love of collecting and art comes from a formal education in the commercial and fine arts and art history. Although my art background served me well in my career as fashion consultant, it found its truest expression in more private pursuits.

I have continued to paint and sketch through the years with very modest success—I refer to my work being of the "kitchen" school, meant to be displayed on the refrigerator with a magnet alongside the kids' drawings. And I have pursued collecting with a passion curtailed only by the limits of my finances—and my husband's protestations of "enough." He often reminds me that it only took a few trips with our old Volkswagen van to move our possessions into our first house, and that when we left England many years later, we managed to fill a transatlantic super-container.

My history of cooking and collecting has for some time been seen as the makings of a book by my longtime friend Joel Avirom, the creative director for *The Artful Chicken*. He, along with others who frequently dined at my table and were invariably served chicken, but rarely the same dish twice, thought a cookbook devoted to chicken would be quite refreshing. That was back in the early 1970s. As the years went by and chicken became the preferred meat of America, Joel continued to encourage me with the suggestion that I make the cookbook something special with my own signature.

Two favorite possessions in my chicken collection—a pair of antique prints from Cassell's *Book of Poultry* pur-

chased in a market in Cambridgeshire, England, and a Ukrainian decorated Easter egg from my grandmother—inspired me to combine the delicious with the delightful as a collection of recipes and art objects.

This book is meant as a celebration of the fine food and art of the chicken and intended for all who appreciate its charm. I hope you take as much pleasure from reading, viewing, and cooking from this book as I did in creating it.

Over the years of cooking chicken dishes and collecting chicken objects, and certainly since I began this book, I have acquired the nickname "the chicken lady." I am often offered hostess or birthday gifts of chicken objects that range from the sublime to the ridiculous. Friends invariably send me clippings of new or unusual chicken recipes and they almost always write little notes of thanks, birthday greetings, or recipes on cards decorated with chickens.

Part of my chicken collection is displayed on a tray in the entrance hall of my home. Included are cards, notes, and even stamps decorated with images of chickens in original designs or based on antique prints, folk paintings, or museum works. In the righthand corner sit a ceramic rooster and hen acquired during one of my habitual flea-market visits.

THE CHICKEN IN HISTORY

Poultry is for the cook what canvas is to the painter. It is served to us boiled, roasted, fried, hot or cold, whole or in pieces, with or without sauce, boned, skinned, stuffed and always with equal success.

—JEAN ANTHELME BRILLAT-SAVARIN, NINETEENTH-CENTURY FRENCH GASTRONOME

MORE THAN 100 YEARS LATER, MONSIEUR SAVARIN'S words could not be more true. Chicken today is as popular a food as it is a popular visual for art and both the food and the art are equally diverse in preparation or presentation.

The modern chicken's most ancient ancestors are said to be a breed of wild fowl that inhabited the jungles of India, Malaysia, and China. The domestication of these birds probably began sometime around 5000 B.C. by the people of the Indus valley, but the domesticated chicken first arrived in the Western world in Greece in the fifth century B.C. The popularity of the chicken as a domestic animal spread quickly throughout the world and, as today, it was appreciated for its meat, eggs, and even its feathers.

In ancient Rome, chickens were not just presented cooked at table. Some were offered as sacrifices to the Roman gods, while certain chickens were considered sacred and viewed as oracles—the patterns of their pecking and scratching for grain were used for divination.

The capon was also a creation of ancient Rome. To conserve grain, a law was passed in 162 B.C. that forbid the consumption of fattened hens (or pullets, as they have been known). Since the neutering of either sex increases the chicken's size and weight considerably, poulty breeders resorted to castrating their roosters rather than spaying their hens. Thus was "born" the capon, which allowed the Romans to abide by the law and still have plump chickens on their tables. The pullet, which had enjoyed some popularity in France since the fourteenth century, more or less disappeared in the eighteenth century, while the capon is still available today.

For most of the Middle Ages, poultry of all types was seen as to the feudal

ABOVE: *A Greek vessel circa 500 B.C.*
OPPOSITE: *The fancy Victorian nesting hen covered dish is of glazed earthenware with gold detailing that suggests it is Jackfield ware from Staffordshire. The black finish was produced by adding manganese to the clay as well as to the glaze. The statuette also is Staffordshire china. A nineteenth-century barnyard portrait and crackled glaze give an old look to a new tray; a reproduction Grecian bowl holds wood and stone eggs.*

The chicken first arrived in the Western world around the fifth century B.C. in Greece and was quickly taken into the farmyard fold of domesticated fowl and animals. Both the Greeks and the Romans used the chicken for consumption and ritual. The image of the cock is often represented on their coins.

For the Greeks the rooster could be connected to different divinities because of his own varied traits. Those that linked him to rebirth or resurrection and sunrise and pugnacity or healing associated the cock to gods with similar attributes such as Zeus, Persephone, Apollo, Ares, Athena, Hermes, and Aesculapius. The esteemed bird was also offered as a gift of love.

ABOVE: Detail from the Greek red-figured krater, or vessel, on the preceding page. The scene depicts Ganymede carrying a rooster. According to the myth, this Trojan youth was abducted by Zeus and taken to Mount Olympus where he was made cupbearer for the gods and became immortal. The inclusion of the rooster in this image can be understood as a reference to Zeus or perhaps the cock as a gift offering of love and tribute to the gods.

OPPOSITE: A cock and hen scratching for food is the scene depicted in a Roman fresco. The image could refer to a barnyard scene of simple domesticity created as a pictoral vignette painted as interior decoration for a villa. Alternately, the cock scratching at seeds or grains could refer to the practice of reading the resulting patterns. Roman officials looked for guidance in such scratchings.

lord's manor or castle born. While part of the everyday diet, it was also an important element of banquets at which food was served to many guests in elaborate presentations. Although the table service that was provided and the table manners that prevailed would be considered primitive and crude by today's standards, these banquets are said to have been the power meals of their day.

Diners used their own daggers to cut up a roasted chicken presented to as few as one or as many as three other dinner companions seated at a section of the hall's long table. The two or four configuration was called a "cover," which today is a restaurant term for the number of individual diners it serves as well as the origin of "cover charge." The diners were given a square cut of stale bread, measuring about 4 by 6 inches and called a trencher, to use as a plate. They could eat the chicken off the tips of their daggers or with their fingers. Wooden squares with a slight depression in their center replaced the bread "plate" around the fifteenth century, but forks did not come into common use until the beginning of the eighteenth century. What the table service lacked in style was made up by the presentation of numerous cooked dishes.

The dish of a pie containing live birds such as the one described in the nursery rhyme of "Four-and-twenty blackbirds baked in a pie" is a rather good, and possibly true, example of the level of extravagance achieved, even for the humble chicken, at these meals. Cooked fowl, presented with its feathers reapplied and placed on fabulous serving pieces, might be set within an elaborate floral arrangement; various roasted poultry might actually be offered stuffed one within the other from smaller to larger.

Certainly the importance of the visual presentation of food has continued over the centuries, often as opulent and on as grand a scale until more recent times. Today diners at one of the celebrated grand restaurants may experience with pleasure the arrival of their dishes carried by as many waiters as there are people seated at their table, topped by silver domes that are simultaneously whisked off in one dramatic movement—but they would be appalled if they found live birds singing on their plates instead of just the roasted poussin. They might very well encounter a whole poached bird complete with head and feet in some traditional French restaurants, but most commonly, decorative garnishes range from simple sprigs of fresh herbs to cut and carved vegetables or fruits to accent dishes even at the humblest of eating establishments. Edible flowers are easily gotten, even from many supermarkets, to decorate the most modest chicken dish at home.

The importance of presentation in home entertaining has spawned entire industries for decorations and accessories for the table, dining room, and even kitchen for hundreds of years. Whether that entertaining is lavish or casual, the modern host can find advice and inspiration from books, magazines, and even consultants; an enormous selection is offered by shops, catalogues, or the internet to create an impressive table. The art of the chicken as a decorative object has benefited from this long-term trend.

To be sure, more mundane and practical ways of preparing and presenting chicken existed during the Middle Ages and were used or followed for centuries; some are seen even today. The ready-cooked spit-roasted chicken that can be purchased today from food shops and supermarkets

finds historic links with those cooked on braziers and sold in the rue de la Huchette in Paris, a practice that continued there from the medieval period until the days of the French Revolution. A variety of traditional poached chicken dishes can find their beginnings in the medieval iron cauldron perpetually suspended over a fire, its contents—broth, vegetables, uncooked or leftover meats—replenished daily.

History has even produced celebrity, if not celebratory, chicken dishes. Napoleon's chef is supposed to have created a dish with chicken, tomatoes, crayfish, and eggs on an Austrian battlefield to commemorate France's victory in 1800. The dish—Chicken Marengo or less than authentic versions (the eggs are generally omitted)—can still be found in recipe books. The famous chef Georges Auguste Escoffier (1846–1935) created Chicken Jeanette, a cold dish of stuffed chicken breast served on a ship carved out of ice, after the doomed ship *Jeanette* was crushed by icebergs. A less chilling idea was the creation of a chicken specialty to sing the praises of opera diva Luisa Tetrazzini—a combination of chicken and spaghetti in a parmesan and sherry cream sauce with a breadcrumb topping called Chicken Tetrazzini.

There are also famous breeds of chickens, so celebrated for their excellence that cooking with them perceivably enhances the dishes in which they are used. Chickens from Bresse, France, the region northeast of the lush vineyards of Burgundy, are held in such high regard that in the late 1950s the nation's parliament granted them the *appellation d'origine controlée*, a regulatory quality title usually reserved for wines or cheeses. Raised on a diet of corn soaked in milk, Bresse chickens freely roam in an enclosure of not less than an acre shared by no more than 500 chickens. French regulation requires a minimum of 10 square yards for each bird. The *poulets de Bresse* are actually quite patriotic. Not only do they carry a special tricolor tag and seal, symbolizing the blue, white and red of the French flag as part of their packaging, but the birds themselves naturally sport the tricolor with their blue feet, white plumage, and fire red combs. Chefs have been known to pay up to $400 for the top Bresse bird at a competition that has been held since 1862.

For thousands of years and the world over, the chicken and its egg have also been appreciated as spiritual or religious symbols. Ancient eastern and western cultures, societies, and religions have shown the cock as representing the sun, the dawn, light and enlightenment, life and resurrection in art, literature, rituals and beliefs, all because of his natural attribute of crowing at daybreak and welcoming the dawn. The regularity and reliabilty of the cock's daily performance and the confident manner in which he carries it out, has earned him the qualities of vigilance and courageousness as well. As an ancient or primitive symbol the hen most often turns up in associations with the underworld and with spirits; her later symbolic significance represents mothering care, and with that, charity. The hen and the egg both quite naturally have associations with the origins of life and the beginning of the world. The egg however, is far and away the most revered and common symbol of rebirth or resurrection.

Chicken is so popular today that the marketplace supports a great variety and demands a great deal of quality. Nutritional and environmental concerns—and perhaps some culinary demands—have dramatically altered the chicken that is available in the market today. There has been a revival of the grain-fed, antibiotic-free, and free-roaming poultry of the old-style farmyard (though this may be simulated on a grander scale for mass production of a specialist kind). Whatever the chicken selected, there is an abundance of choice as to the packaged cuts available that was unheard of as recently as twenty-five years ago and certainly when M. Savarin declared the versatility and variety of chicken.

Through the ages chicken—cock, hen, chick, and egg—has provided us with food not just for the table, but food for thought and art as well.

OPPOSITE: *A Wedgewood platter carries a pattern called "Golden Cockerel" that has stylistic connections with Asia in both the theme and design. It was a gift of thanks and a tribute for numerous chicken dishes from a friend. This plate started me off on my chicken collecting.*

The Artful
Chicken

1

Roast & Bake

ALTHOUGH CHICKEN LENDS ITSELF PERFECTLY TO many methods and techniques of cooking, roasting is the one that shows off its naturally good qualities to the best advantage. In my opinion, there is nothing as delicious, nor as simple to prepare, as a roast chicken. If asked to say the first thing that pops into my head in association with the word "chicken," I would have to say "roast." It *is* simply delicious.

Roasting and baking are essentially the same method with very subtle differences and, these days, the distinction is less hard and fast. In both techniques, food is cooked in currents of hot, dry air circulating in some sort of an oven. Roasting usually refers to the cooking of a whole bird (or other whole meats), while baking generally implies the cooking of parts, as well as minced meats (such as meat loaf) and fish. Dishes that are cooked in the oven without the addition of any liquid and enclosed in a container, such as a covered roasting pan, clay pot, or Dutch oven, are also considered to be baked.

So which came first, roasting or baking? If you believe man had his first "home-cooked" food approximately half a million years ago when a piece of meat accidentally fell into his open fire, then grilling came before both roasting and baking. Only later did man begin to develop these slower cooking methods, which protected his food from the flames of the open fire.

Cooking meat in the embers of a fire or in a pit, on a flat stone to the side of the fire, on a spear well above the fire, or encased in mud or leaves are probably the earliest cooking techniques—and they have changed little over the millennia. It was discovered in the eighteenth century that Australian Aborigines, who are considered to be direct descendants of the *Homo sapiens* who lived in 30,000 B.C., still cooked small animals and birds in coatings of clay.

In the medieval period, meats—and a considerable proportion of these were poultry—were roasted and baked in open fires in the centers of great halls or in huge hearths; in warm months, cooking sheds were used. Later, niches in the walls of the hearth or fireplace

Fine artists, drawn to the chicken's colorful visual and symbolic imagery, have represented this creature in their paintings throughout the centuries. In Listening to the Cockerel (1944) and other works, Marc Chagall celebrates the artful chicken in a rich and imaginative composition.

were developed as cooking spaces away from the flames: these might have been the first true ovens. Next came the primitive brick oven, which was heated with coal and needed to be raked out after each use. It would have been considered state of the art in most homes and continued in wide use until the early nineteenth century.

Certainly cooking in these brick ovens was a contest of skills. The only controls were the distance of the heat source from the food and the cooking time, which made roasting or baking in these ovens a dicey enterprise. However, even in today's high-tech ovens nothing is foolproof. As accurate and well-maintained as you might think your oven is, it is best to take its temperature—often, if not every time you prepare one of the recipes in this chapter.

Use a good-quality oven thermometer, set squarely in the middle of your oven. If the temperature that it registers does not match your oven's temperature setting, increase or decrease the setting accordingly. Do not try to adjust the cooking time. With very few exceptions to this rule, never roast or bake a cold chicken in a cold oven: the chicken should be room temperature and the oven preheated to the correct setting. Let whole birds rest after the roasting or baking is finished before you carve them.

The recipes that follow include whole roasted birds, big and small; whole birds baked in closed clay or iron pots; and baked pieces, minced meats, and a pie. All are simple, as this method of cooking should be, incorporating easy ways to add distinguishing flavors to create a variety of tastes—spice rubs, marinades, stuffings under the skin, glazes, or breaded coatings and sauces.

Four-Herb Chicken

*Black Olive Baked Chicken Thighs
with Tomato Purée*

Madame Arnaud's Roast Chicken

Anchovy Roasted Cornish Hens

Sweet Onion Roasted Chicken

Rosemary, Lemon & Garlic Roasted Poussins

Baked "Southern-Fried" Chicken

Honey & Lavender Baked Chicken Legs

Baked Basil & Pastis Chicken

Clay Pot-Baked Chicken & Garlic

Maple Syrup Cornish Hens

Pot-Roasted Chicken & Vegetables

Asian-American Spiced Baked Chicken

*Chicken Meat Loaf
with Tomato & Rosemary Sauce*

*Foccacia-Breaded Thighs
with Mustard Sauce*

Mashed Potato Baked Chicken Pie

Four-Herb Chicken

SERVINGS: 4

The herbs used here—parsley, sage, rosemary, and thyme—are as classic to chicken dishes as the Simon & Garfunkel song of the same name is to the 1960s. The herbs are used outside, inside, and under the skin.

An adjustable roasting rack is used in the roasting pan.

4½-pound whole free-range roaster
Sea salt
Freshly ground pepper
1 sprig fresh flat-leaf parsley
1 sprig fresh rosemary
1 sprig fresh thyme
4 or 5 fresh whole sage leaves
2 tablespoons minced fresh flat-leaf parsley
2 tablespoons minced fresh sage
2 tablespoons minced fresh rosemary
2 tablespoons minced fresh thyme
4 teaspoons olive oil
Paprika

Preheat the oven to 450 degrees, setting the rack at the middle level.

Season the cavity of the bird with salt, pepper, the sprigs of fresh herbs, and the whole sage leaves.

Combine the minced herbs in a small bowl and stir in the olive oil. Gently loosen the skin over the breast and thighs and spread the herb mixture over the flesh and under the skin (see Note).

Season the outside with salt, pepper, and paprika.

Place the chicken, breast side up, on the adjustable roasting rack in a roasting pan and put it in the oven. Roast for 10 minutes, then turn the chicken on one side and roast for 10 minutes. Turn the chicken onto the other side and roast for another 10 minutes.

Lower the temperature to 350 degrees and continue roasting for 15 minutes. Turn the chicken to the first side, and roast for 15 minutes. Turn the chicken breast side up and finish roasting for 30 to 35 minutes or until done (see page 162).

Transfer the chicken to a board and let it rest for 10 to 15 minutes before carving.

Note: To stuff under the skin of the chicken, first use your fingers to separate the skin from the flesh underneath, taking care not to poke holes through the skin. Place small amounts of the stuffing into the opening as far as possible. From the skin side, work the stuffing up and about, spreading it as far and as evenly as you can, adding additional small amounts as you go until the stuffing is used up.

Suggested Wine: Côtes du Rhône, such as Saint-Joseph

Black Olive Baked Chicken Thighs with Tomato Purée

SERVINGS: 4

*H*ere is a common variation on a Mediterranean theme, this time played out on pieces rather than whole chickens. Pass the tomato purée at the table. Sautéed broccoli rabe makes a nice accompaniment.

2 cloves garlic, crushed through a garlic press

1 cup oil-cured (Moroccan-style) black olives, pitted and minced

½ cup fresh parsley leaves, minced

1 teaspoon hot red pepper flakes, crushed or coarsely ground

2 tablespoons olive oil

8 chicken thighs

Sea salt

Cracked black pepper

Preheat the oven to 450 degrees, setting the rack at the middle level.

Combine the garlic, olives, parsley, red pepper flakes, and 1 tablespoon of the oil in a mixing bowl and blend to a thick paste.

Gently loosen the skin of the chicken thighs and spread the paste under the skin (see Note, page 6). Rub the pieces with the remaining olive oil and season with salt and pepper.

Place the thighs on a flat rack set in a roasting pan and put in the oven.

Lower the heat to 375 degrees and bake for 40 to 45 minutes or until done (see page 162).

Serve with a shaker of hot red pepper flakes for a more spicy dish.

Suggested Wine: Dolcetto d'Alba

Tomato Purée

2 cups fresh tomatoes (about 4 medium tomatoes), peeled, seeded, and chopped (or canned and well drained)

1 tablespoon olive oil

Sea salt

Freshly ground pepper

Combine the ingredients in a food processor and blend to a thick sauce. Serve at room temperature or just slightly warmed.

*M*ugs and cups offer an easy and affordable way to start a collection that is as much fun as it is functional. An interesting collection can be defined, refined, and later expanded by focusing on a single specific element or combination of elements such as shape, color, size, material, period of design style, or motif.

In my case, chicken motifs rule the roost including this collection of mugs and cups that I have acquired over the years. I enjoy drinking my morning coffee from them as well as using them as containers for fresh herbs such as parsley, sage, rosemary, and thyme. Kitchen shears are at hand in a mug with a colorfully hand-painted rooster from Hungary. The sage is in an Irish mug depicting cute baby chicks and mother hen placed within a bordered medallion design and rendered in a naif manner. Rosemary tops the rooster, hand painted in a design style considered historically traditional to Italian ceramics; the porcelain mug holding thyme features a hen in the style of antique paintings of the same genre. The likeness is repeated on the inside lip. The parsley's container presents a rooster that could be related to those from antique poultry prints while placing him in a landscape that could only be associated with a more modern style.

Madame Arnaud's Roast Chicken

SERVINGS: 6

Roast chicken and a potato gratin were the traditional Sunday afternoon dinner prepared by my mother-in-law when my husband was a boy. He helped with the preparations of the meal and fondly remembers the work and the pleasure of quiet Sundays, the house full of tantalizing cooking aromas. Steamed and buttered *haricots verts* often completed the main course; green beans or spinach are equally appropriate.

When we lived in London, I roasted the famous French chickens from Bresse, which deserve their reputation for excellence, or corn-fed chickens. Now that I am back home in the States, I look for free-range or organically fed roasters. As today's chickens are younger and generally leaner than those available to my mother-in-law, I have adjusted the cooking method accordingly. But the heart of this simple recipe, which makes a comforting home-style meal, comes from Andrée Canova Arnaud of Grenoble, France, and is true in every way to her spirit.

An adjustable roasting rack is used. Two ovens are ideal for the different timing and temperatures required for the chicken and the potato gratin. Otherwise, the gratin can be made ahead and reheated just before serving.

The table for a family Sunday dinner is presented with as much tradition as the meal being served—roast chicken, potato gratin, and haricots verts followed by cheese and a dessert. The dinner should be a feast for the eyes as well as the stomach.

A tablecloth with a traditional toile de Jouy print center and border features chickens in both. It makes a fitting backdrop for the family's best tableware and serving pieces.

The Italian hand-painted porcelain rooster shaped vase is life-size, making it tall enough to hold a bouquet of hydrangeas, which are fresh from the garden.

5½- to 6-pound whole free-range roaster
Kosher or coarse sea salt
Cracked black pepper
4 sprigs fresh thyme
1 tablespoon unsalted butter, softened
½ cup chicken broth or stock
½ cup dry red wine
1 large carrot, scrubbed and cut into chunks
1 medium onion, cut into ¼-inch slices
1 tablespoon of unsalted butter (optional)

Preheat the oven to 450 degrees, setting the rack at the middle level.

Season the cavity of the chicken with salt, pepper, and 2 sprigs of the thyme. Rub the outside with the softened butter and season with salt, pepper, and the leaves of the remaining sprigs of thyme.

Combine the broth and wine in a measuring cup or pitcher. Scatter the carrot chunks and onion slices on the bottom of a roasting pan.

Place the chicken breast side up on the adjustable roasting rack and set it in the pan. Roast for 10 minutes.

Baste with about 2 tablespoons of the wine and broth mixture and turn the chicken on its side. Baste, and roast for 10 minutes. Baste again and turn the chicken on its other side. Baste, and roast for an additional 10 minutes.

(continued)

Lower the temperature to 350 degrees, baste again, and roast for 15 minutes. Baste, turn the chicken onto its other side, and continue roasting for 15 minutes.

Turn the chicken breast side up and baste. Continue roasting for an additional 40 to 50 minutes or until done, basting every 10 to 15 minutes (see page 162).

Transfer the chicken to a carving board and let it rest for 10 to 15 minutes.

Pour the accumulated cooking juices and vegetables from the roasting pan into a small saucepan, add the pat of butter, and place over low heat, keeping the mixture warm.

Carve the chicken and arrange the pieces on a serving platter. Pour the sauce through a fine sieve, pressing down on the vegetables to extract the liquid, into a warmed sauce boat. Pass the sauce at the table.

Suggested Wine: Côte de Beaune

Potato Gratin

Position an aluminum foil baking sheet or shallow pan on the floor of the oven under the gratin dish to minimize the clean-up if the liquid in the gratin overflows.

The gratin can be made ahead and reheated. Leftover gratin *réchauffé* (fried to reheat) in butter in a skillet or sauté pan is considered a delicacy in our house!

Butter for the dish
1 clove garlic, cut in half
4 large (2½ pounds) Yukon Gold
*   potatoes, peeled, thinly sliced, washed,*
*   and placed in a bowl of cold water*
4 to 6 cloves garlic, peeled
Sea salt
Freshly ground pepper
Flour
3 to 4 tablespoons unsalted butter
4 or more cups whole milk

Preheat the oven to 450 degrees, setting the rack in the lower middle shelf.

Butter a large baking dish (approximately 9 by 13 inches, or similarly proportioned oval) and rub with the cut garlic clove. Remove about one third of the potato slices from the water, dry them thoroughly, and place them, overlapping, over the bottom of the dish. Depending on taste, crush one or two garlic cloves through a press directly over the potato slices, distributing the pulp as evenly as possible. Season with salt and pepper and sprinkle about 1 tablespoon plus 1 teaspoon of flour over the layer as evenly as possible. Dot the layer with 1 tablespoon of the butter. Repeat the process, making successive layers until the ingredients are used up and the dish is almost filled to the top. You should have three or four layers.

Pull out the oven rack and place the baking dish on it. Pour in the milk to just cover the top layer; add more if needed. Gently push the rack back into

the oven. Bake for 15 minutes or until the milk just begins to bubble.

Lower the heat to 350 degrees and cook for an additional 40 minutes, or until the potatoes are very tender when pierced by a fork and the top of the gratin is golden.

A white rooster has special significance in more than one culture. In Islamic writings, the prophet Muhammad praises this bird: "The white cock is my friend: he is the enemy of the enemies of God."

To the Chinese, the white cock can, among other things, represent purity of heart. The belief is behind the custom, at Chinese weddings, of the bride and groom eating white sugar cocks.

Anchovy Roasted Cornish Hens

SERVINGS: 3 TO 6

*I*n the Arnaud family a discussion of what ingredients and their combinations make a dish traditionally Provençal, Niçoise, or northern or southern Italian can be as interminable as the one about the chicken and the egg. When anchovies, olives, tomatoes, basil, capers, and even peppers or eggplant or zucchini are in some way combined and are dominant features in a dish, it is hard to find all in agreement as to which descriptive is truly accurate.

Geopolitical and social history aside, these ingredients, which unquestionably dominated much of Mediterranean cuisine for centuries, produce some of the greatest tasting, most varied, healthful, and easy-to-prepare dishes there are.

One long-standing "Provençal" tradition marries the tangy flavor of anchovies with chicken roasted in the oven or over a fire. Some family recipes include salt pork or a soft cheese—or both—in the stuffing, which makes it extra succulent. And the most authentic version would call for salted anchovies rather than those packed in oil. Here, however, anchovies in oil work quite well.

The servings will vary from one-half to one whole bird for each guest, depending on appetites and the rest of your menu.

1 tablespoon anchovy paste
4 ounces anchovy fillets, drained
   and mashed
3 tablespoons minced flat-leaf parsley
2 tablespoons unsalted butter, softened
3 whole Cornish hens
Freshly ground pepper
Olive oil

Preheat the oven to 450 degrees, setting the rack at the middle level.

Combine the anchovy paste, anchovy fillets, and parsley with the butter and, using a fork, mash to a paste.

Season the cavities of the birds with pepper. Gently loosen the skin over the breast and thigh areas and spread the paste under the skin (see Note, page 6). Rub the outsides of the hens with oil and season with pepper.

Arrange the hens breast side up on a flat rack in a roasting pan, and place in the oven. Roast for 10 minutes.

Turn each bird on one side and roast for 10 minutes, then turn them onto the other side and roast for an additional 10 minutes.

Lower the temperature to 350 degrees and continue roasting for 10 minutes. Turn the birds onto the other side and finish roasting for 10 to 15 minutes or until done (see page 162).

Serve with sautéed cherry tomatoes, small bowls of Niçoise olives, and caper berries at the table.

Suggested Wine: Mercurey

*R*eproductions and adaptions of a variety of antique print techniques and styles frequently appear on contemporary fabrics for the home. This scenic design, printed for placemats and napkins, captures the refined detail of engraving in its rendering of a handsome cock.

Sweet Onion Roasted Chicken

SERVINGS: 4

I usually serve this with a confit of endive and onions, which my husband adores. This dish is excellent even if served at room temperature or chilled.

An adjustable roasting rack is used in the roasting pan.

1 Vidalia onion, or other variety of sweet onion

4 tablespoons unsalted butter, softened

¼ teaspoon sweet paprika, plus additional

4½-pound whole free-range roaster

¼ teaspoon brown sugar

Sea salt

Cracked black pepper

Olive oil

Preheat the oven to 450 degrees, setting the rack at the middle level.

Cut the onion in half and mince one of the halves. In a mixing bowl, blend the minced onion, butter, and ¼ teaspoon of paprika into a paste.

Season the cavity of the bird with the brown sugar, salt, and black pepper. Place the remaining half onion in the cavity.

Gently loosen the skin over the breast and thighs and spread the onion and butter paste under the skin (see Note, page 6). Rub the outside of the bird with olive oil, season with salt and pepper, and sprinkle with additional paprika.

Place the chicken, with the breast side up, on an adjustable roasting rack in a roasting pan and put in the oven. Roast for 10 minutes, then turn the chicken on one side and roast for 10 minutes. Turn the chicken onto the other side and roast for an additional 10 minutes.

Lower the oven temperature to 350 degrees and continue roasting for 15 minutes. Turn the chicken to the first side, and roast for 15 minutes. Turn the chicken breast side up and finish roasting for 30 to 35 minutes or until done (see page 162).

Transfer the chicken to a board and let it rest for 10 to 15 minutes before carving.

Suggested Wine: Fleurie

During the eighteenth century, figurative or symbolic motifs, rather than the printed word, were widely used to publicize or advertise. Minimal and graphic in design and direct in their messages, these flat silhouettes, painted panels, or three-dimensional sculptures were the dominant form of advertising. The use of word-printed signage became more prevalent as the literacy rate rose.

Of course, nothing was more appropriate for advertising a poultry or egg farm and accompanying shop than a rooster sign, posted outside or hanging above, to announce the sale of farm-fresh chickens, eggs, or both. These simple silhouettes, cut from wood or metal in the shape of the bird, were always of an eye-catching size and usually decoratively painted. In the nineteenth century, these signs began to include words, which were painted, printed, or chalk-drawn.

This huge crowing cock, a nineteenth-century French shop sign, is painted on both sides. The small hen silhouette to the left is stamped out of metal, in imitation of early signage. Below, from left to right, are three wooden hen cut-outs: the first hen and egg is free-standing folk art; the 1920s hen lawn ornament was sponge-painted; and a modern artisan, Barbara Dove Kenian, handcrafted the checkerboard chicken, which functions as a doorstop.

The nineteenth-century French basket was designed to take chickens to and from the market. Ropes were threaded through the rings around the basket's edges to secure the live birds.

Rosemary, Lemon & Garlic Roasted Poussins

SERVINGS: 3 TO 6

These three flavors in combination are classic for roasting chicken throughout Italy. Italian cooking seems to present this dish as a simple basic, with all three ingredients used to stuff the cavity, and the rosemary and lemon used again to season the outside. I like to intensify tastes by stuffing the ingredients under the skin as well.

The servings will vary from one-half to one whole bird for each guest, depending on appetites and the rest of your menu.

1½ lemons
3 whole poussins
Sea salt
Freshly ground pepper
3 sprigs fresh rosemary
3 cloves garlic, peeled
3 cloves garlic, peeled and finely slivered
3 tablespoons fresh rosemary leaves
Olive oil
Lemon pepper

Preheat the oven to 450 degrees, setting the rack at the middle level.

Peel and thinly slice the half lemon. Cut the whole lemon into four quarters.

Season the cavities of the poussins with salt and pepper and stuff each with 1 peeled garlic clove, 1 sprig rosemary, and 1 unpeeled lemon quarter.

Gently loosen the skin over the breast area, and insert a few garlic slivers, rosemary leaves, and lemon slices between the skin and the flesh (see Note, page 6).

Rub the outsides of the birds with olive oil, squeeze the remaining quarter lemon over the tops; sprinkle with lemon pepper and any remaining rosemary leaves.

Arrange the poussins in a roasting pan, breast side up, place in the oven, and lower the heat to 375 degrees. Roast for 10 minutes. Turn the poussins breast side down and roast for 15 minutes. Turn the poussins breast side up again and continue to roast for 10 to 15 minutes or until done (see page 162).

Suggested Wine: Barolo

Decorative sprigs of rosemary enhance the presentation of these poussins, which have been roasted with the fragrant herb, along with lemon and garlic. The linen tea towel is woven with a rooster motif, and a glimpse of the toile de Jouy tablecloth reveals a farm scene with chickens.

Toile de Jouy is an antique printed fabric named after the Royal Factory of Jouy, once located in Jouy-en-Josas near Versailles, France. The factory first produced the fabric in the late eighteenth century. Its signature look was created from precisely drawn and detailed designs reproduced through a printing technique involving copper sheets or plates (and, later, carved copper rolls). The use of a single color—red, blue, green—printed on a natural-colored ground is the most classic.

Often the landscape or figures selected for the toile de Jouy patterns represented farmyard scenes, peasants, or animals. The chicken in its natural habitat was and is frequently the subject of this fabric. The toile style is reproduced today as simple one-color designs or prints, which employ an additional color for the ground.

FOLLOWING PAGES: A vivid red rooster design—in the toile de Jouy style—decorates the cotton fabric that will serve as a tablecloth for this picnic. A cushion printed with a farmyard scene featuring a rooster and a hen, caters to today's taste for country charm.

Baked "Southern-Fried" Chicken

SERVINGS: 6 TO 8

Here the Southern classic is baked without sacrificing the crunchy, crisp coating and succulent interior. This cuts some of the calories and fat, but if you are really serious, remove the skin before breading.

The seasoning used for the bread crumbs incorporates the classic combination for chicken: rosemary, lemon, and garlic. I like to serve this with Southern-style vegetables, such as mustard or collard greens or kale, and grits.

For an even less fattening version, boneless, skinless breasts can be used. Adjust the cooking time to 20 to 25 minutes. For breasts with the bone in (with or without skin), bake for 30 minutes.

Olive oil

2 cups dry unseasoned bread crumbs

5 tablespoons plus 1 teaspoon minced fresh rosemary

1½ teaspoons sea salt

1 teaspoon freshly ground black pepper

2 tablespoons lemon pepper

2 teaspoons granulated garlic

1 tablespoon minced fresh lemon zest

6 large chicken thighs

6 large chicken drumsticks

Flour

2 eggs, lightly beaten with a little water

Preheat the oven to 400 degrees, setting the rack at the middle level.

Lightly coat a baking sheet with olive oil.

Mix the bread crumbs with the rosemary, salt, pepper, lemon pepper, garlic, and lemon zest.

Dredge the chicken pieces in the flour, then dip them into the egg mixture, letting the excess run off. Roll the chicken in the bread crumbs to coat them thoroughly.

Arrange the chicken on the baking sheet and put it in the oven. Bake for 40 to 45 minutes or until done (see page 162), turning over once halfway through the cooking time.

Suggested Wine: Light Burgundy, such as Beaujolais

LEFT: *This graphic and abstract ceramic hen plate is by Alison Palmer, who individually handcrafts her spirited designs from white earthenware clay and lead-free glazes.*

OPPOSITE: *Colorful and bold shapes are favored by Melinda K. Hall, an artist and one-time chef who has celebrated the chicken in the arts of both painting and cuisine.*

Honey & Lavender Baked Chicken Legs

*M*y memories of our frequent travels in the south of France focus on a mix of very particular fragrances and flavors: herbs and spices that signify the cooking of the region as well as others that are not necessarily associated with food. This recipe is inspired by my memories and a delightful meal we once enjoyed at a small restaurant near fragrant lavender fields in Provence. The chef presented a refreshing scoop of lavender and honey sorbet as the intermezzo, to clean our palates between our appetizers and the main course of grilled chicken. I first made this recipe after returning to London from a family visit in the south, toting a new supply of honey from my sister-in-law's beehives, fresh lavender, and dried lavender buds.

½ cup honey
1 teaspoon fresh lavender leaves
1 teaspoon fresh thyme leaves
4 whole chicken legs
2 cloves garlic, slivered
4 sprigs fresh thyme
4 sprigs fresh lavender
Sea salt
Freshly ground pepper
2 to 3 teaspoons dried lavender buds
Additional honey or unprocessed
    raw honey (see Note)
Kosher or coarse sea salt
Cracked black pepper

Preheat the oven to 450 degrees, setting the rack at the middle level.

Combine the honey and lavender and thyme leaves in a mixing bowl.

Gently loosen the skin of the chicken legs over the thigh areas and insert a sliver of garlic, a sprig of thyme, and a sprig of lavender under the skin of each piece (see Note, page 6). Season the legs with salt and pepper on both sides.

Spoon the honey mixture over each chicken leg to coat. Place the pieces in a baking dish that will hold them in one layer.

Place the dish in the oven and bake for 15 minutes. Baste and turn. Bake for 10 minutes, then turn and baste. Bake another 10 to 15 minutes or until done (see page 162).

Remove the sprigs of lavender and thyme from under the skin. Place on a serving platter or individual plates and sprinkle the rims with the lavender buds. Pass the honey, cracked pepper, and kosher salt at the table.

Note: If you can get some honey still in the comb, it makes the presentation at the table more interesting.

Suggested Wine: Australian Syrah

ABOVE: *A wildly fanciful scene of chickens on parade adorns an Easter postcard.*

OPPOSITE: *Chicken, honey, and lavender complement each other—in both this recipe and the table setting. Dried lavender buds decorate the rim of the plate and fresh-cut sprigs of lavender fill an English teapot of highly imaginative design. The chicken is served with a combination of wild and long-grained rice and red onions baked in red wine.*

Baked Basil & Pastis Chicken

SERVINGS: 4

*T*his recipe was developed by my husband's uncle, Yves Auzolle, especially for this book. He incorporated two traditional elements from the south of France to flavor this chicken dish: fresh basil and pastis. Pastis is an anise-flavored liqueur of a caramel color usually served as an aperitif (one part liquor to five parts water), which turns it a beautiful creamy yellow. I cannot think of a sleepy town in provincial France during the summer without imagining its square, surrounded by shady plane trees and sidewalk cafés, and men enjoying their pastis while playing *boules* on the village center's dusty court. Pastis is as traditional a symbol of France as are a beret and a baguette.

The dish is marinated overnight.

1 cup dry white wine
1 tablespoon plus 1 teaspoon pastis
28 large fresh basil leaves
1 medium-sized sweet onion, finely sliced
3 cloves garlic, crushed with the
*   flat of a knife*
Sea salt
Freshly ground pepper
3¼-pound whole free-range roaster, cut
*   into quarters*
Olive oil

Combine the wine, pastis, 20 basil leaves, onion, garlic, salt, and pepper in a shallow porcelain or glass baking or serving dish. Add the chicken pieces, turn them several times to coat, and leave them in the dish skin side up. Cover the dish tightly with plastic wrap and refrigerate overnight.

Remove the dish from the refrigerator. Turn the pieces skin side down, re-cover the dish, and let the chicken come to room temperature, about 30 minutes.

Preheat the oven to 450 degrees, setting the rack at the middle level.

Remove the chicken pieces from the dish. Strain the marinade through a sieve into a measuring cup or pitcher and reserve.

Place the chicken pieces in a non-reactive baking dish. Drizzle each with some olive oil and top each with 2 large fresh basil leaves. Place the dish in the oven. Lower the temperature to 375 degrees and bake for 45 to 50 minutes or until done (see page 162), basting with the reserved marinade from time to time.

Suggested Wine: St. Vérans

ABOVE: *A* 1958 copy of Chicken Little is part of my library of nostalgia. The chicken has delighted readers for centuries in charming stories, many of which make a moral or educational point. In Aesop's Fables, Le Roman de Renart, the Canterbury Tales, and the much more recent Chicken Little, rooster, hens, and chicks are colorful characters that make fools and examples of themselves.

OPPOSITE: *Modern glassware nesting hens like the one in front are often made from old molds and are available in a variety of colors. This one is of iridescent green.*

A Staffordshire pottery hen dates from the mid-1800s.

Clay Pot–Baked Chicken & Garlic

SERVINGS: 4

This old French recipe is known as *poulet aux 40 gousses d'ail* (chicken with 40 garlic cloves). The chicken and the unpeeled garlic are cooked on a bed of classic herbs enclosed in a clay pot or enameled cast-iron Dutch oven, often hermetically sealed with a band of dough. Given the recipe's utter simplicity, it produces an amazingly flavorful and succulent dish—and it's foolproof.

Over the years, I have made this in a plain cast-iron pot, an enameled iron Dutch oven, and most recently a clay pot. My ovens have varied from electric to circotherm and convection, to my current ordinary gas oven. I have used medium to large birds. The dish always comes out right. My latest version is baked in a clay pot and substitutes elephant garlic cloves, reducing the number of cloves necessary and making the garlic more a vegetable than a condiment. You might want to offer toasted slices of a rustic country or sourdough bread on which to spread the roasted garlic, along with olive oil and a shaker of hot red pepper flakes.

A clay pot is needed. Follow the manufacturer's instructions for the exact cooking temperature and timing.

The centuries-old belief that garlic wards off evil spirits and demons may now be considered a superstition, but garlic's association with certian curative properties and physical wellness continues.

This clay pot, perfect for baking chicken and garlic, is banded with highly stylized reliefs of chickens. The terra cotta tile at far right, meant for warming bread, depicts a rooster welcoming the sunrise. The stoneware crock imitates the salt-glazed exteriors and cobalt blue designs characteristic of eighteenth-century crocks, which often featured birds, especially chickens.

The kitchen towel and pot holders are printed with or cut out as roosters, hens, chicks, and eggs.

3½-pound whole free-range roaster
Sea salt
Freshly ground pepper
3 sprigs fresh thyme
1 clove elephant garlic, crushed with the flat of a knife
12 cloves elephant garlic, unpeeled (or as many as you like)
3 sprigs fresh rosemary
3 sprigs fresh oregano 3 sprigs fresh sage
3 sprigs fresh parsley

2 bay leaves
1 tablespoon coarse salt
1 tablespoon cracked black pepper

Soak the clay pot in cold water for 20 minutes.

Season the cavity of the chicken with salt and pepper and stuff it with the sprigs of thyme and the garlic clove.

Scatter some of the unpeeled garlic cloves and the rosemary, oregano, sage, parsley, and bay leaves across the bottom of the clay pot.

Place the chicken on top of the bed of herbs and garlic. Season the chicken with the coarse salt and the cracked black pepper and arrange the remaining garlic cloves around the chicken.

Cover the pot securely and place in a cold oven. Set the oven temperature to 450 degrees and bake for 1½ hours or until done (see page 162).

Suggested Wine: Red burgundy

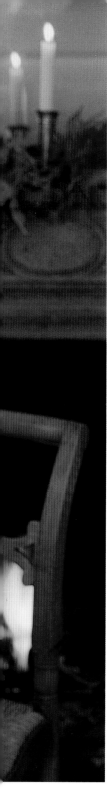

Maple Syrup Cornish Hens

SERVINGS: 8

Thanksgiving is my favorite time in the kitchen. When I moved to London in the late seventies (where the third Thursday of November is not a national holiday), I had to recreate the festivities myself. My first annual celebratory feast was planned for the Saturday following Thanksgiving. I spent a week preparing all the fixings for an American regional holiday meal (the fresh turkey and cranberries were special-ordered from Harrod's elite food halls) and decorating the house with dried Indian corn and tacky pop-up paper turkeys. Each subsequent Thanksgiving we spent in England we explored the regional cuisines of the United States—from New England to Louisiana to the Southwest. Now back in the United States, I've learned to adapt these turkey dishes to chicken so that friends from around the world who visit our home in the countryside of New York State can enjoy Thanksgiving dinner at other times of the year. Here is one of their favorite versions. The cranberry sauce should be made a day or two ahead. The stuffing is cooked separately. For contrast serve with tangy pickled vegetables, like onions, beets, and baby carrots, which can be prepared several days before.

Cornish hens glazed with maple syrup, accompanied by a spicy cranberry sauce and cranberry-apple-yam stuffing (see page 28 for recipes) create a meal as festive as any Thanksgiving dinner.

Autumnal colors—russets, reds, ochres—and a chicken theme unify this well-decorated dining room. The fireplace mantel, where candles glow, is festooned with fall leaves and a modern pair of rooster and hen figurines. Carved wooden chicken-shaped candlesticks and another pair of china figurines, these from the 1930s, form the centerpiece of this bountiful table. The tablecloth and napkins have outline and figurative prints of chickens.

1½ Macoun, Empire Red,
   or McIntosh apples, peeled and
   cored, 1 quartered, ½ minced
4 tablespoons unsalted butter, softened
4 whole Cornish hens
Sea salt
Cracked black pepper
4 sprigs fresh thyme
4 small cloves garlic, crushed
   with the flat of a knife
Olive oil
8 tablespoons maple syrup,
   of good quality
4 teaspoons brown sugar

Preheat the oven to 450 degrees, setting the rack at the middle level.

Combine the minced apple and butter in a bowl and blend together until smooth. Loosen the skin over the breast of each hen and insert 1 tablespoon of the apple mixture into each (see Note, page 6). Using your fingers on the outside, press gently to distribute the mixture evenly.

Season the cavities of the hens with salt and pepper, and stuff each with a sprig of thyme, a clove of garlic, and one apple quarter.

Rub the skin of each hen with a little oil and about 1 tablespoon of the maple syrup.

Arrange the hens breast side up on a flat rack in a roasting pan, and place the pan in the oven. Roast for 10 minutes. Baste with some maple syrup.

(continued)

Turn each bird on one side and roast for 10 minutes. Baste, then turn the birds onto the other side and roast for another 10 minutes. Baste again.

Lower the temperature to 350 degrees and continue roasting for 10 minutes. Sprinkle the hens with half of the brown sugar.

Turn the birds on the other side, sprinkle with the remaining brown sugar, and finish roasting for 10 minutes or until done (see page 162).

Remove the birds from the oven and let them rest for 8 to 10 minutes before cutting in half to serve.

Suggested Wine: Cabernet Sauvignon

Spicy Cranberry Sauce

This recipe is based on one that appeared in a Thanksgiving issue of *Bon Appétit* magazine. The sauce should be made at least a day in advance of serving, to allow the flavors to develop. Leftovers will keep well in the refrigerator for several days.

¾ cup cranberry juice

⅜ cup honey

½ tablespoon grated orange zest

½ stick cinnamon

1 small bay leaf

½ teaspoon grated fresh ginger

¼ teaspoon ground coriander

¼ teaspoon kosher or coarse salt

¼ teaspoon freshly ground black pepper

Pinch or two of cayenne pepper

6 ounces fresh cranberries (½ 12-ounce bag)

2 orange sections, peeled

Combine the juice, honey, and orange zest in a medium saucepan and bring to a simmer; cook for 5 minutes. Add the cinnamon, bay leaf, ginger, salt, black pepper, and cayenne pepper and simmer for 5 minutes.

Add the cranberries and continue simmering, stirring occasionally, until the berries burst and the sauce becomes thick.

Remove from the heat and add the orange sections. Let the sauce cool, then store it in the refrigerator for a least one day. Bring to room temperature before serving.

Cranberry-Apple-Yam Stuffing

¾ pound yams, peeled and cut into 1-inch cubes

¾ pound turkey sausage meat

3 tablespoons unsalted butter

3 Macoun, Empire Red, or McIntosh apples, peeled, cored, and cut into chunks

¾ cup chopped onion

1 tablespoon finely chopped garlic

½ cup chopped celery

½ teaspoon sea salt

Freshly ground pepper

2 tablespoons chopped fresh thyme

1 tablespoon chopped fresh sage

12 ounces fresh cranberries

1½ cups stale sourdough bread cubes, crusts removed

¾ cup dry coarse bread crumbs

3 tablespoons maple syrup

2 cups chicken broth or stock

Preheat the oven to 350 degrees, setting the rack at the middle level.

Cook the yams in a pot of boiling water for 3 minutes. Drain and set aside.

In a nonstick sauté pan, lightly brown the sausage meat, stirring to crumble the meat; transfer the sausage to a large bowl.

Heat 2 tablespoons of the butter in the pan and add the apples, onions, garlic, celery, salt, pepper, and 2 teaspoons each of the thyme and sage. Sauté until the onions are translucent. Remove the pan from the heat and mix in the cranberries.

Add the contents of the pan to the bowl with the sausage meat; add the yams and bread cubes, and mix thoroughly.

Add the remaining thyme and sage, the bread crumbs, and maple syrup and season with salt and pepper. Combine well.

Transfer the stuffing to a deep baking dish and pour the broth over. Cover the dish and bake for 35 to 40 minutes, or until apples and bread cubes are soft.

Uncover, dot with the remaining tablespoon of butter, and bake for 15 minutes longer; the top should be crisp and lightly browned.

Pot-Roasted Chicken & Vegetables

Cast-iron cookware dates back to the times of cooking over an open fire in a fireplace. Like clay, iron conducts heat well and seals in the natural moisture of the contents, resulting in rich and flavorful one-pot meals. This recipe came with the pot, along with instructions for its care, as a gift from Uncle Yves.

A large, well-seasoned and well-maintained cast-iron pot is needed. Alternatively, a clay pot can be used; follow the cooking procedure of the manufacturer or as provided in the recipe for Clay Pot–Baked Chicken and Garlic (see page 24). Alternative vegetables may include peeled sweet potato or yam cut into large chunks, corn on the cob cut into 3-inch pieces, or unpeeled elephant garlic cloves.

3½-pound whole free-range roaster
Sea salt
Freshly ground pepper
4 or 5 sprigs fresh thyme
2 cloves garlic, crushed with the flat
   of a knife
Olive oil
4 small sweet onions, peeled
2 medium leeks, trimmed leaving 2 to 3
   inches of green, thoroughly washed
6 medium carrots, tops trimmed, peeled
   or scrubbed as necessary
4 medium potatoes, scrubbed
2 medium parsnips, tops trimmed,
   peeled (optional)
French cornichons
Kosher or coarse sea salt
Cracked black pepper

Preheat the oven to 450 degrees. Set the oven rack to allow for air space above and below the pot, as close to the middle level as possible.

Season the cavity of the chicken with salt and pepper and stuff it with the sprigs of thyme and the garlic. Rub the outside with oil and season with salt and pepper. (If you like your chicken with a golden skin, brown it on all sides in a bit of oil in a nonstick sauté pan at this point.)

Make a bed using some of the vegetables in a large cast-iron pot, place the chicken on top, and scatter the rest of the vegetables around and over the chicken.

Cover the pot and roast for 1½ hours or until the chicken is done (see page 162) and the vegetables are tender.

Remove the chicken from the pot to a board and let it stand before carving.

Meanwhile, arrange the vegetables on a warm serving platter, cutting the leeks and parsnips into four portions. Keep the vegetables warm while carving the chicken, then serve. Pour any cooking juices from the pot into a small gravy boat or pitcher and pass at the table, along with the cornichons and bowls of coarse salt and cracked black pepper.

Suggested Wine: Slightly chilled red Beaujolais, such as Fleurie

In Norse mythology, the rooster is considered a symbol of vigilance and protectiveness because he perches atop an ash tree to warn of imminent enemy attack. Here, a rooster figure stands on a little bank, perhaps as a security guard.

Asian-American Spiced Baked Chicken

Servings: 4

ABOVE: *This lively rooster paper cutting, perhaps meant to be used as an embroidery pattern, resembles the fearless cock of the Chinese zodiac. In that context, he is considered to be courageous and warlike, as well as a representation of warmth and life in the universe.*

OPPOSITE: *Blue-and-white ceramics hold universal and timeless appeal. This oversized serving platter is a charming example of these classic wares. The rooster and landscape are rendered in a style reminiscent of the Chinese pictorial tradition.*

First produced during the Tang dynasty (618 to 906), China's blue-and-white pottery is referred to as quinghua, *which means "blue decoration." Cobalt blue designs are painted onto white ware, then finished with a clear colorless glaze.*

China's blue-and-white pottery was created in differing styles to cater to the needs and tastes of either the home or export markets. Over the centuries, both types found their way into Europe and created a lasting influence on Western design. Today blue-and-white ceramics in Asian designs and chinoiserie motifs are as popular as ever in new versions, faithful reproductions, or as treasured antiques.

This dish was inspired by two marvelous food tales. The first story, an ancient one, is of a highway robber in China who stole a chicken from a nearby farm. He was roasting it over an open-pit fire when he heard approaching footsteps. Fearing discovery and arrest, he wrapped the bird in leaves and hid the evidence by burying it under the coals. Later, after being released from custody, he returned to the spot, dug up, unwrapped, and tasted the stolen chicken. He found it to be cooked to perfection.

Of more recent origin is the family story of Tom Hope of Chatham, New York, and his father, Fred, of West Virginia, from the days of the Great Depression. Fred, like many other men in the 1930s, was reduced to the life of a hobo, living around the railroads and in boxcars. These hobos were not above stealing food if they could not barter their odd-job skills in exchange for a meal or its fixings. A true prize would be a chicken. They would kill the bird and clean out the entrails, leaving the feathers on. After completely encasing the bird in mud, they baked it on an open fire. When broken open, the feathers came away with the baked mud casing.

The highway robber's serendipitous meal, universally known as "beggar's chicken," has evolved into a much more sophisticated dish. The chicken has a stuffing of meat, aromatic mushrooms, and tangy pickled vegetables; it is wrapped in lotus leaves and coated in mud. The oven-baked clay casing is cracked open with a hammer and the leaves removed at the table.

Here, a clay pot is used to achieve a similar result. Follow the manufacturer's instructions for the exact cooking temperature and timing.

3½-pound whole free-range chicken

1 teaspoon sea salt

½ teaspoon cracked Szechuan
    peppercorns

6 sprigs fresh cilantro

4 cloves garlic, 3 crushed with the flat
    of a knife, 1 chopped

1 1-inch piece cinnamon stick

1 tablespoon fresh ginger, peeled
    and chopped (peelings reserved)

2 tablespoons coarsely chopped
    fresh cilantro

1 tablespoon peanut oil

1 tablespoon soy sauce

⅛ teaspoon ground cinnamon

⅛ teaspoon ground ginger

1 teaspoon granulated garlic

1 teaspoon ground coriander

¼ teaspoon curry powder

Soak the clay pot in cold
water for 20 minutes.

Season the cavity
of the chicken with
¼ teaspoon of the salt
and ¼ teaspoon of the
Szechuan pepper, and
stuff with the sprigs of
cilantro, the crushed garlic, cinnamon stick, and
ginger peelings.

Mix the chopped cilantro,
chopped garlic, and fresh ginger
with a little oil and dash of soy
sauce in a bowl. Gently loosen the

skin of the chicken, insert the mixture,
and spread it over the breast and down
to the leg (see Note, page 6).

Combine the dry spices and the rest
of the salt and pepper in a small bowl.
Rub the outside of the chicken with the
rest of the oil and drizzle the rest of the
soy sauce all over. Sprinkle the spice
mixture over.

Place the chicken in the clay pot.
Cover the pot securely and place in a

cold oven. Set the oven temperature to
450 degrees and bake for 1½ hours or
until done (see page 162). Remove
from the oven, uncover, and let the
chicken stand for 10 to 15 minutes.
Set the chicken on a carving board,
pour the cooking juices from the pot
into a gravy boat or small pitcher, and
serve at the table.

Suggested Wine: California or
Australian Chardonnay

Chicken Meat Loaf with Tomato & Rosemary Sauce

SERVINGS: 6 TO 8

Nothing is more traditional to American home-style cooking than meat loaf and gravy. In the 1950s, moms across the country were famous for this dish, which they served frequently, more often than not with mashed potatoes and peas. In the nineties, a nostalgia for the warmth and welcome of home resulted in a trend called "comfort food," which glorifies the nurturing spirit of old-fashioned family meals and stick-to-your-ribs dishes like this one.

Vegetable oil

¾ pound ground chicken (preferably light and dark meat mixed)

¾ pound ground turkey (preferably light and dark meat mixed)

¾ pound ground pork

1 egg, lightly beaten

½ cup whole milk

2 teaspoons white wine Worcestershire sauce

1 cup fine bread crumbs

4 tablespoons minced fresh cilantro

3 tablespoons minced sweet onion

1 tablespoon garlic crushed through a garlic press

2 teaspoons Kosher or sea salt

½ teaspoon freshly ground pepper

Preheat the oven to 350 degrees, setting the rack at the middle level. Line a roasting pan with heavy-duty aluminum foil and lightly oil the bottom and sides.

Combine all of the remaining ingredients and thoroughly mix them together. Shape the mixture into a loaf and place it in the prepared pan.

Bake for 1 hour or until done (juices will run clear). Turn off the oven and let stand for 10 minutes with the door open.

Tomato & Rosemary Sauce

1 cup chicken broth or stock

2 teaspoons shallots, minced

½ cup dry white wine

2½ cups diced fresh or canned tomatoes, peeled and drained

1 teaspoon tomato paste

4 sprigs fresh rosemary

1¼ cups crème fraîche or sour cream

Pour the broth into a saucepan and add the shallots, white wine, tomatoes, tomato paste, and rosemary. Bring to a boil and cook until the liquid is reduced by about half. Remove from the heat and remove and discard the rosemary sprigs.

Transfer the sauce to a food processor, blend until smooth, then pass it through a fine sieve back into the saucepan.

Place over medium-high heat and bring to a simmer, lower the heat, add the crème fraîche, and simmer for about 5 minutes, stirring from time to time. Do not let the sauce boil.

Pour the sauce into a gravy boat or small pitcher and serve with the meat loaf at the table.

Suggested Beverages: Beer or Merlot

LEFT: *From the 1950s and still fabulous: a tin serving tray printed with flamboyant fighting cocks holds linen cocktail napkins humorously printed with a rooster, hen, and egg.*

OPPOSITE: *A tea towel printed with a weathercock serves as a cloth for a TV dinner tray. On the shelf stand two preposterously colored and formed folk art chickens from Central and South America.*

Focaccia-Breaded Chicken Thighs with Mustard Sauce

SERVINGS: 4 TO 6

*W*hen traveling through the Burgundy region of France visiting the vineyards, I enjoyed a chicken dish that had a delicious mustard sauce and a breadcrumb coating on the chicken. I later found a recipe for this classic dish that provided me with the basis for this variation—flavored bread crumbs rather than plain, and thighs only in place of whole legs.

8 large chicken thighs

2 tablespoons flour

2 eggs, lightly beaten

1⅓ cups dry focaccia bread crumbs (see Note)

⅓ cup vegetable oil

2 tablespoons unsalted butter

2 tablespoons shallots, finely chopped

8 ounces (1 cup) crème fraîche or sour cream

2 tablespoons Dijon mustard

⅓ cup chopped chives

Sea salt

Freshly ground pepper

Preheat the oven to 425 degrees, setting the rack at the middle level.

Dredge the chicken thighs in the flour, then dip them into the eggs, letting the excess run off. Roll the thighs in the bread crumbs to coat them thoroughly. Place the thighs on a plate and put them in the refrigerator to chill and set for 8 to 10 minutes.

Heat the oil in a large skillet or sauté pan and brown the chicken thoroughly and evenly on both sides.

Place the chicken in a baking dish and place it in the oven. Lower the temperature to 375 degrees and bake for 25 to 30 minutes or until done (see page 162).

Turn off the oven and open the door, but do not remove the chicken.

Heat the butter in a small skillet, add the shallots, and sauté for 1 to 2 minutes. Turn the heat to low, add the crème fraîche, and stir to combine with the shallots. Add the mustard and chives and stir well to just heat through; do not let the sauce come to a boil.

Place the chicken on a platter, pour the sauce into a sauce boat, and serve at the table.

Note: Day-old—or older—herbed focaccia makes especially tasty crumbs for this dish. Otherwise, make the crumbs from any other bread and season them to taste with dried herbs. Alternatively, make crumbs from seasoned prepared stuffing mix or add herbs to plain prepared crumbs. I sometimes use Williams-Sonoma's Focaccia Country-Style Stuffing, which is seasoned with herbes de Provence.

Suggested Wine: California Cigare Volant

*C*ocky Chef Chanticleer is an amusing addition to any kitchen or pantry. His serving trays could easily support baskets of vegetables or potted herbs.

Mashed Potato Baked Chicken Pie

SERVINGS: 6 TO 8

*T*his is based on the English shepherd's pie, a dish that traditionally incorporates leftovers from Sunday's roast of lamb as its base and fresh mashed and creamed potatoes for the topping. For generations of English families, it was a popular dish at home and a favorite at English pubs. Here, chicken replaces the lamb, and vegetables are added to make this a satisfying one-dish meal.

The recipe suggests using baby portobello mushrooms, which are considerably smaller in size than the regular portobellos and thus require less chopping; however, large ones can be used.

3 to 3½ pounds Yukon Gold potatoes, peeled and quartered

2 tablespoons unsalted butter, softened

Sea salt

Freshly ground pepper

1 cup heavy cream

1 pound ground chicken

1 pound ground pork

3 tablespoons olive oil

1 pound cremini or baby portobello mushroom caps, cut into eighths or small chunks

1 large sweet onion, chopped to yield about 2 cups

½ teaspoon dried thyme

2 teaspoons fresh thyme

1 teaspoon minced fresh sage

2 cloves garlic, minced

1 fresh sage leaf

2 tablespoons flour

¾ cup canned tomatoes, diced and drained

¼ cup chicken broth or stock

1 can baby sweet peas, drained and rinsed

Paprika

Put the potatoes in a saucepan of water, bring to a boil, and cook until very tender, 20 to 25 minutes. Drain in a colander. Rinse the pan and return the potatoes to the pan.

Mash the potatoes together with the butter until smooth. Season with salt and pepper, add the cream, blend well and mash until the potatoes are smooth and creamy. Cover to keep warm.

Mix the chicken and pork together in a bowl and set aside. Preheat the broiler to high.

Heat 1 tablespoon of the oil in a sauté pan over medium-high heat, add the mushrooms, and sauté, stirring from time to time, for 3 to 5 minutes or until lightly browned. Remove the mushrooms from the pan and set aside.

Wipe the pan clean and place it over medium heat. Add the remaining oil, then add the onion, dried and fresh thyme, minced sage, garlic, and the whole sage leaf; cook, stirring from time to time, until the onion is translucent and just soft but not browned.

Raise the heat and add the chicken and pork mixture and lightly brown it, breaking up any lumps and evenly combining the meats with the onion mixture. Sprinkle with the flour, and stir it in; season with salt and pepper. Add the tomatoes and broth, cover, and cook for 5 to 8 minutes or until the sauce has thickened. Remove the pan from the heat and remove and discard the sage leaf.

Drain the mushrooms and add to the meat mixture along with the peas.

Spoon the chicken and vegetable mixture into a large, shallow baking dish (approximately 11 by 15 inches). Top with the potatoes, spreading them to completely cover the chicken mixture as evenly as possible. Create a textured surface using the tines of a fork, drawing across the potato topping in long strokes; sprinkle abundantly with paprika.

Place the dish under the broiler for 8 to 10 minutes until the top is golden.

Suggested Wine: Beaujolais, such as Pisse Dru

2

GRILL &
BROIL

IN AMERICA, GRILLING OR BROILING ARE SAID TO BE the most popular methods of cooking most foods, particularly chicken. It is easy to understand why. The characteristics of grilling and broiling meet the needs of life today. Grilling is convenient and above all fast.

By grilling and broiling, food is cooked by direct, extreme radiant heat and requires no added fat. Food attains a crisp or browned exterior and is cooked through while retaining tenderness and moisture. Whatever the size—small pieces or even whole butterflied birds—the results are equally good. Ideally though, whole birds or joints of meat should be cooked on a rotating spit. There is very little substantial difference, if any, in the distinction between grilling and broiling with the above definition. Grilling is almost synonymous with outdoor cooking on a grid or grill-work of metal bars over hot coals or wood. Gas- and electric-fueled outdoor barbecues, stove-top skillets with grooved surfaces that imitate grill bars, and specially fitted stove-top grills cook in the same manner. Broilers built into stoves cook similarly; the difference is in the added flavor of

A Beswick pottery nesting hen from England perches on a late eighteenth-century American country chair. The use of a color glaze for each part of the dish lid and base, or one color used over all turns out handsome pieces.

charcoal, distinctive wood chips, and their smoke—not to mention the pleasure of cooking outdoors.

Today, grilling is what most of us mean when we say "barbecue," but in strict modern culinary terms barbecue refers to various types of slow cooking that are at the heart of regional cooking from the Carolinas through the Southwest. The food may be buried in a pit or turned on a spit but always cooks for many hours, even overnight.

Time is the principle factor that separates grilling from barbecue: It is far faster. Food—smaller, thinner pieces of it—is cooked over a livelier open wood, charcoal or gas fire, though it might be covered for part or even all of the time.

Our first London house had a garden, and one of my first purchases was a Weber Kettle (purchased at three times the U.S. price). Our new neighbors were mystified to see us outside barbecuing so often, despite unfavorable weather conditions, but barbecuing caught on like wildfire throughout our neighborhood.

If the discovery of the method of grilling—"flame

grilling" in this case—was an ancient happy accident that is subject to both conjecture and controversy, so is the early development of cooking over coals. Discoveries of the remains of fire pits lined with stones are said to be prehistoric ovens; the food was grilled directly over additional stones heated inside. The first spit-grilling is attributed to prehistoric hunters who, once having enjoyed the benefits of cooked meat from the home fires figured out how to skewer it on a spear and mount it over their campfires. And it is most certainly accepted that in the Middle Ages spit-grilling in the open or in the hearth was common. More recent history, from the time of the exploration and colonization of the New World, brings us to the purported origin of the word "barbecue."

Natives on the Spanish-owned island of Hispaniola called their method of cooking over fire *boucan*. The word became *boucanier* in French and transformed into buccaneer, the English word to describe the new inhabitants. The Spanish word describing the wooden structure the native Caribs used was *barbacoa,* which in the end transformed into barbecue.

Grilling and broiling are methods that allow for a great variety of chicken dishes. Small or larger birds can be cooked whole on a spit or split open and flattened. Brochettes or kebabs make wonderful "one-pot dishes" as they allow for the cooking of accompanying vegetables or fruits all in one go. Dry rubs and dry marinades add different and distinctive flavors. Wet marinades also add flavor, seared in by the heat.

The cooking times and temperatures for recipes in this chapter are specific to a covered outdoor gas barbecue with an electric spit, broiled in an oven broiler, or pan-grilled on the stove top; adjustments should be made for other equipment. For spit-grilled recipes, an oven rotisserie can be used.

Spit-Grilled Mustard Chicken

SERVINGS: 4

*F*rom medieval times meat cooked on a spit over an open or hearth fire was a common way to cook large pieces of meat or whole birds. Today electric spits and rotisseries are available to fit most barbecues or can work in home ovens.

In our house the spit-grilled chicken of choice is seasoned with mustard; the combination is as natural and simple as bread and butter. I frequently use plain or flavored mustards (either store-bought or spiced up in my kitchen) for marinating and coating chicken, or simply as a condiment. This recipe uses a spicy mustard with mustard grains, called *moutarde de Meaux*, which is widely available. A rotisserie spit is used on a gas-grill barbecue.

2 tablespoons moutarde de Meaux
2 tablespoons plus 1 teaspoon minced
    flat-leaf parsley
2 tablespoons unsalted butter, softened
4-pound whole free-range roaster
Sea salt
Cracked black pepper

Mix the mustard and parsley together and blend in the butter to form a smooth paste.

Season the cavity of the bird with salt and pepper. Gently loosen the skin over the breast and thighs and spread some of the mustard paste over the flesh and under the skin (see Note, page 6), reserving a teaspoon or so of paste. Let the chicken stand for 1 to 2 hours in the refrigerator. Remove the chicken 20 minutes before cooking.

Preheat the gas grill to high.

Rub the outside of the chicken all over with the remaining mustard paste and season with salt and pepper.

Attach the bird to the spit. Lower the grill temperature to medium and cook the chicken for 30 minutes. Lower the temperature to low and cook for an additional 30 minutes or until done (see page 162).

Suggested Wine: Chianti Classico, served very slightly chilled

OPPOSITE: *A new Italian ceramic serving platter with a central rooster motif and free-form floral border is hand painted.*

*F*or centuries, the Black Rooster has been the emblem of Italy's Chianti region.

The origin of this symbol is an ancient legend. During the Middle Ages, a border rivalry existed between the Italian city-states of Florence and Sienna. To bring about peace, it was decided to settle their differences with a contest rather than a battle.

Each city would choose its best horseman. On the appointed morning, each rider would set out when the cock crowed to penetrate as deeply as possible into the the disputed territory. The point at which the horsemen met would thereafter mark the border between the city-states.

Having chosen their riders, the cities looked to the roosters who would, in effect, be the alarm clocks, the starting shots, for the event. It is said that the Sienese selected a handsome white rooster, plump and content, having been well fed and coddled, while the Florentines picked a scrawny black rooster who was always hungry and scratching for food.

Perhaps the black rooster's hunger drove him to rise early, for he crowed well before dawn on the day of the contest, giving the Florentine horseman a good start over Siena's. The Florentine rode to within ten miles of Siena before meeting with its horse and rider. As a result, the boundary drawn by the encounter left most of the Chianti Classico region under the authority of the Florentine Republic. The black rooster was rewarded for his efforts with the honor of becoming the trademark of the region's wine consortium.

0.750   CHIANTI CLASSICO CHIANTICLASSICO CONSORZIO   0.750

AL 4761067

Cornish Hens with
Sun-Dried Tomato & Arugula Pesto

—🐓—

SERVINGS: 4 TO 6

This recipe, like the other outdoor grilling recipes in this chapter, is prepared on a gas grill, which is a slower grilling method than charcoal. A rotisserie spit, attached to the grill, is used.

Fresh basil can be substituted for the arugula.

6 tablespoons sun-dried tomatoes
  (not packed in oil), rehydrated
  in water, patted dry, and chopped

2 tablespoons minced arugula

2 teaspoons chopped pignoli

1 tablespoon chopped garlic

½ teaspoon salt

2 tablespoons olive oil, plus additional

4 whole Cornish hens

Sea salt

Freshly ground pepper

Mix the sun-dried tomatoes, arugula, pignoli, garlic, and salt together in a food processor, add the 2 tablespoons of oil, and blend to a paste.

Season the cavities of the birds with salt and pepper. Gently loosen the skin over the breasts and spread the paste over the flesh, little by little working it over the breasts and down to the thighs (see Note, page 6).

Preheat the gas grill to high.

Rub the outsides of the hens with oil, and season with salt and pepper.

Attach the hens to the spit. Lower the temperature to medium heat and cook the hens for 20 minutes.

Reduce the heat to low and cook for an additional 20 to 25 minutes or until done (see page 162).

Suggested Wine:
Red Saumur

LEFT: *B*old roosters cast in brass were popular in the latter part of the nineteenth century. A small statuette with Asian stylized feathers is from India. The jaunty brass cock mounted on a wooden platform is from France. It serves as an inkwell, opening at the neck for access to ink. The large cock's head, also from France, circa 1860s, is quite a novelty. When one presses down on its beak, a bell mechanism is engaged. Its original purpose was to "ring" for the servants.

RIGHT: The statuette, also brass, was a desktop ornament or promotional gift for Pathé Frère, a French company founded by Charles Pathé in 1869. It dominated the film business worldwide until Holly-wood and Kodak surpassed it in the late 1920s. Pathé Fréres was involved in production and sales of movies, cameras, projectors, and film; it was the originator of the movie newsreel and the weekly adventure serials that became popular in the U.S. The origin of the cock as an emblem of France goes back to ancient Roman times. It's based on a Latin pun that plays on the word gallus, which translates as both "Gaul" and "cock" (meaning rooster).

Curry Barbecued Chicken Breasts

SERVINGS: 6

*T*he inspiration for this dish comes from Indian tandoori cooking. The meat is marinated in yogurt flavored with classic curry spices. This recipe, and the other outdoor grilling recipes in this chapter, is prepared on a gas grill, which is a slower grilling method than charcoal.

4 whole chicken breasts, boned and skinned.

3 cups (24 ounces) whole-milk yogurt

3 cloves elephant garlic, crushed through a garlic press

3 tablespoons desiccated coconut

2 tablespoons plus 1 teaspoon grated fresh ginger

2 tablespoons finely chopped fresh cilantro

2 tablespoons mild curry powder

½ teaspoon sea salt

Cut the chicken breasts in half lengthwise, then in half crosswise, and pierce a few times on each side with a fork.

Mix the yogurt, garlic, coconut, ginger, cilantro, and curry powder and salt in a non-reactive baking dish large enough to hold the chicken breasts in one layer. Place the chicken into the mixture and then turn the pieces over two or three times to coat them evenly on both sides. Cover the dish and place it in the refrigerator for at least 3 hours or overnight.

Remove the chicken from the refrigerator and bring to room temperature.

Preheat the gas grill to high.

Cook the breasts over high heat for 5 minutes on each side. Lower the heat to medium and cook the breasts for 5 minutes more on each side or until done (see page 162).

Suggested Beverage: Cabernet Sauvignon or beer

At cock's crow the sun rises again—the darkness retreats, the world awakens and the spirit is reborn. The rooster's most common, timeless, and universal associations are based on his announcing the dawn of the new day. This daily routine imbues him with the qualities of reliability, vigilance, and protectiveness, which are represented in some of the most ancient cultures and religions; it also relates to various religious stories of resurrection of the spirit and the illumination of the soul. The cock was connected to the gods of ancient Greece, Islam, the Hindus, Shintos, Zoroastrians, and early Christians by this link with the sun.

In the Bible, Jesus warns an unbelieving Peter that he will deny their association— not once, but three times before the cock crows. From this came a symbolic relationship of St. Peter and the rooster—and, in time, clocks. The story inspired the image of the rooster to signify St. Peter in fine and decorative arts; St. Peter also is the patron saint of watch and clockmakers. These references come together in this French desk clock that dates from between 1860 and 1880.

There were other religious connections made through art. The story of the cock and St. Peter was frequently portrayed on early Christian sarcophagi as a warning against arrogance. It also became an iconographic reference to repentance for the early Christians, because Peter was said to have wept in remorse for his action. And it must be through these associations with repentance that the rooster came to be commonly used on eighteenth-century gravemarkers in America.

OPPOSITE: *A colorful Italian ceramic statuette in the form of the crowing cock.*

Honey-Mustard Grilled Chicken Breasts

SERVINGS: 4

This recipe, and the other outdoor grilling recipes in this chapter, is prepared on a gas grill, which is a slower grilling method than charcoal.

2 tablespoons honey
3 tablespoons Dijon mustard
2 tablespoons finely chopped
    flat-leaf parsley
2 whole chicken breasts, boned
    and skinned, halved (4 pieces)
Sea salt
Freshly ground pepper

Combine the honey, mustard, and parsley in a bowl.

Pierce the breasts a few times on each side and arrange them in a shallow nonreactive baking dish. Spoon 1 tablespoon of the honey mixture on each of the pieces, and turn to coat them thoroughly. Reserve the remaining marinade.

Let the chicken marinate for 1 hour in the refrigerator.

Bring the chicken back to room temperature and season with salt and pepper.

Preheat the gas grill to high.

Place the chicken on the grill and cook over high heat for 5 minutes on each side. Lower the heat to medium; brush the chicken pieces with the reserved marinade on both sides and cook for an additional 5 minutes on each side or until done (see page 162). Drizzle with the remaining honey-mustard mixture.

Suggested Wine: Syrah

The rooster seems always to have been the more popular publicized chicken, as this French nineteenth-century sign, cut in metal and detailed with paint, would indicate. The sign features the cock as an advertising symbol for the sale of eggs, though the hen would have been a more natural and likely association.

Basil Vinaigrette Grilled Chicken Breasts

SERVINGS: 4

Flavorful salad dressings make excellent marinades. This is just one of many we use in preparing chicken for outdoor grilling. A perfect side dish would be slices of broiled or grilled tomatoes topped with melted mozzarella cheese and drizzled with olive oil at the table.

This recipe, like the other outdoor grilling recipes in this chapter, is prepared on a gas grill, which is a slower grilling method than charcoal.

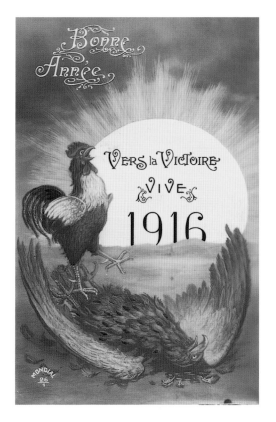

¾ cup olive oil

3 tablespoons red wine vinegar

1 tablespoon Dijon mustard

¼ teaspoon sea salt

Freshly ground pepper

2 whole chicken breasts, boned
     and skinned, halved (4 pieces)

2 tablespoons chopped fresh basil

8 whole basil leaves (optional)

The French have the tradition of sending greeting cards for the New Year. This one has special significance, wishing a Happy 1916 and expressing hope for a French victory over Germany. A truly new dawn. The cock is the national symbol of France while the fallen eagle represents Germany. The end of WWI did not come until two years later.

Whisk together the oil, vinegar, mustard, salt, and pepper to taste in a bowl to make a vinaigrette.

Pierce the breasts a few times on each side and arrange them in a shallow nonreactive baking dish. Spoon 1 tablespoon of the vinaigrette over each piece, and turn to coat them well. Sprinkle the chicken breasts with 1½ tablespoons of the chopped basil. Add the remaining basil to the remaining vinaigrette and reserve. Let the chicken marinate for 30 minutes.

Drain the excess marinade from the chicken.

Preheat the gas grill to high. Cook the chicken over high heat for 5 minutes on each side. Lower the heat to medium. Brush the chicken pieces with some of the reserved marinade and grill for about 5 minutes more on each side until done (see page 162).

Serve each piece topped with some of the reserved dressing and 2 basil leaves.

Suggested Wine: Dry white, such as a French Chardonnay or California Sauvignon Blanc

Chili-Cinnamon Pan-Grilled Cutlets

SERVINGS: 4 TO 6

*T*his recipe is based on a beef dish I enjoyed at the Inn of the Anasazi in Santa Fe, New Mexico, which combined chili powder and cinnamon as a rub for filet mignon. With my preference for chicken, I couldn't wait to try adapting those spices to a simple pan-grill recipe.

1 tablespoon plus 1 teaspoon chili powder

1 tablespoon plus 1 teaspoon ground cinnamon

½ teaspoon salt

½ teaspoon dried oregano

3 whole chicken breasts, boned and skinned, halved and pounded to ⅛-inch thickness (6 pieces)

Mix the chili powder, cinnamon, salt, and oregano together in a small bowl.

Sprinkle the chicken pieces with the mixture on both sides and let stand for 30 minutes.

Heat a stove-top grill pan or cast-iron skillet over medium-high heat. Grill the chicken pieces until golden and cooked through, 3 to 4 minutes per side or until done (see page 162).

Suggested Wine: Sparkling white wine *méthode champenoise* such as Gruet

The plates shown here may be new, but they are hand turned and painted in the tradition of rooster designs that have decorated ceramic tableware for centuries. This pattern, originally favored by the French and English, is often called after its literary ancestor, "Chanticleer." He was a heroic but vainglorious rooster whose close and near fatal encounter with a clever but equally conceited fox is the subject of two similar medieval stories—one in Le Roman de Renart, created by French clerics between 1170 and 1250, the other in Chaucer's Canterbury Tales, written between 1387 and 1400. The ceramic pattern is usually a colorful and painterly rendering of a stylized cock, presented with a jaunty air or crowing.

The rooster pattern table linens also are hand painted. And two of an antique set of varying sized covered china dishes—fashioned as a nesting basket for the bottom and a pile of eggs with a cheeky chick hatching for the cover— are set out just for show, while the third and largest dish holds a pepper accompaniment.

Grilled Chicken Breasts with Spicy Green Olive Tapenade

SERVINGS: 4

For a very Mediterranean-style meal, accompany this dish with individual slices cut from a Parmesan cheese–flavored polenta cake lightly grilled on the barbecue.

This recipe, like the other outdoor grilling recipes in this chapter, is prepared on a gas grill, which is a slower grilling method than charcoal.

1 cup green olives, pitted and chopped
2 cloves garlic, chopped
1 teaspoon hot red pepper flakes
½ teaspoon salt
2 tablespoons olive oil, plus additional

2 whole chicken breasts, halved (4 pieces)
Sea salt
Freshly ground pepper

Preheat the gas grill to high.

Mix the olives, garlic, red pepper flakes, and salt together in a food processor, add the 2 tablespoons of oil, and blend to a paste.

Gently loosen the skin over the breasts, and spread the paste over the flesh and under the skin, working it over the breasts (see Note, page 6).

Rub the outsides of the breasts with oil, and season with salt and pepper.

Cook the chicken over high heat for 5 minutes on each side. Lower the heat to medium and cook the chicken pieces for about 5 minutes on each side or until done (see page 162).

Suggested Wine: Red Côte de Provence

Drumsticks Grilled with Lemon Herbes de Provence

SERVINGS: 4

*H*erbes de Provence is a mix of herbs that can be found, under various brands, in the spice sections of supermarkets and specialty stores. Lemon pepper is another ready-to-use combination. Grilled zucchini slices, seasoned with some of the herbes de Provence and sprinkled with freshly cracked black pepper and drizzled with olive oil, makes a nice side dish for this simple meal.

This recipe, like the other outdoor grilling recipes in this chapter, is prepared on a gas grill, which is a slower grilling method than charcoal.

4 tablespoons herbes de Provence
3 tablespoons lemon pepper
1 teaspoon sea salt
2 tablespoons minced lemon zest
2 teaspoons granulated garlic
6 to 8 chicken drumsticks
Juice of 1 lemon

Mix the herbs de Provence, lemon pepper, salt, lemon zest, and garlic together in a small bowl.

Place the drumsticks in a nonreactive shallow baking dish, pour the lemon juice over the pieces, then sprinkle the herb mixture under the skin (see Note, page 6) and on the skin. Let stand for 30 minutes.

Preheat the gas grill to high. Cook the drumsticks over high heat for 5 minutes on each side. Lower the heat to medium and cook the drumsticks for an additional 15 minutes or until done (see page 162), turning once or twice.

Suggested Wine: White Côte de Provence

An assembly of chicken miniatures or "putz," molded from composition substances and hand painted are of German origin.

With the exception of the box topped with a baby chick, which was for candy, the collection is made up of individual toys and figures from different toy sets. The themes of the sets could have been play farms or Noah's Arks.

The framed print that hangs above is a page from Cassell's Book of Poultry, depicting the first place prize winner of the 1871 fair at Birmingham, England.

The artist is the celebrated Robert Ludlow and the bird that is immortalized in this lithograph is named Psyche, a Dark Brahma pullet or fattened hen (or female version of the capon) owned by a Mr. L. Wright.

Apple Brandy & Peppercorn Broiled Chicken Legs

SERVINGS: 4

Like the classic Chicken Normandy Style (see page 119) this dish is inspired by the traditional cooking of this region in northern France, which draws on apples and apple products.

4 tablespoons calvados or Armagnac

3 tablespoons green peppercorns preserved in vinegar, drained and minced

½ cup heavy cream

¼ teaspoon sea salt

4 chicken legs

4 tablespoons heavy cream (optional; see Note)

Mix the calvados, peppercorns, cream, and salt together in a shallow dish. Pierce the chicken legs a few times on both sides. Place them in the dish, turning to coat thoroughly. Let the chicken marinate for 3 hours or overnight, turning once or twice.

Return the chicken legs to room temperature. Preheat the broiler to high.

Transfer the chicken legs to a broiler pan lined with aluminum foil, shaking off the excess marinade; reserve the marinade if you are making a sauce (see Note).

Broil the legs top side down for 12 minutes, turn them over, and cook for another 10 to 12 minutes or until done (see page 162). Arrange the chicken with the Broiled Apples on a platter and serve.

Note: For a sauce, put 2 to 3 tablespoons of reserved marinade in a small saucepan, bring to a boil for 1 to 2 minutes, then stir in 4 tablespoons of cream. Remove from the heat and keep warm for serving.

Suggested Beverage: A French cider or dry red wine from the Loire Valley, such as Bourgueil

Broiled Apples

2 tablespoons calvados or Armagnac

2 tablespoons honey

2 Macoun or other tart red apples, peeled, cored, and halved

2 Golden Delicious apples, peeled, cored, and halved

Sea salt

Freshly ground pepper

For designers of interiors and home furnishings, the image of the chicken is an icon of their romanticized view of country living. American and European homes have been decorated for decades with all manner of chicken image objects in the attempt to capture the tranquility of provincial life.

Here, a cozy corner looks just right for pursuing pastimes like reading or needlepoint. Two tapestry cushions are homemade achievements from needlepoint kits of nineteenth-century designs. The glass tumbler ornamented with a strutting rooster is thought to be from the 1940s.

The table lamp has a turned mahogany wooden shaft and bottom, the ceramic polychrome glazed base is in the form of a rooster and thought to have been commercially produced in the 1940s. The cloth is in the style of colored lithographs illustrating fancy breed roosters; the glass coaster also has a printed rooster design.

Preheat the broiler to high.

Combine the calvados and honey and brush the apple sections with it.

Arrange the apples in a shallow flameproof baking dish and season with salt and pepper. Broil for 10 to 15 minutes until nicely golden brown, and tender but not soft.

Note: If you are using just one broiler, prepare the apples first and keep them warm while you broil the chicken.

Green Chile Broiled Chicken Thighs

SERVINGS: 4 TO 6

Chiles are a classic and popular ingredient in the traditional cooking of the Southwest. In this recipe, the chiles for the stuffing are rather mild, so I like to turn up the heat a little by serving a side dish of medium-hot peppers stuffed with Monterey Jack cheese and baked. The frozen margaritas can cool things down again!

1 (4-ounce) can diced mild green chiles

2 tablespoons chopped fresh cilantro

1 clove elephant garlic, chopped

½ teaspoon salt

1 tablespoon olive oil, plus additional

6 large chicken thighs, about
    1½ pounds total

Sea salt

Hot red pepper flakes

Preheat the broiler to high.

Mix the chiles, cilantro, garlic, and salt in a food processor, add the 1 tablespoon of oil, and blend to a paste.

Gently loosen the skin over the thighs at one end and spread the paste over the flesh and under the skin, working it over the thighs (see Note, page 6).

Brush oil over the skin and season with sea salt and a light sprinkling of red pepper flakes.

Place the thighs skin side down on a broiler pan lined with aluminum foil and broil for 10 minutes. Turn the thighs over and broil for an additional 10 minutes or until done (see page 162).

Suggested Beverage:
Frozen margaritas

OPPOSITE: *In a pose reminiscent of the majestic American Bald Eagle holding arrows, a chicken clutching sheaves of wheat in its claws serves as a symbol for peaceful agrarian patriotism. The image is woven on a rug made in Maine in the 1880s.*

BELOW: *In some states during the 1880s and 1890s—especially during Grover Cleveland's presidential campaign—the rooster served as the emblem of the Democratic party. This tin rooster silhouette might have topped a flagpole flying the Star-Spangled Banner or the Democratic party's standard during late nineteenth-century political rallies.*

Orange-Ginger Tamari
Chicken Thighs

SERVINGS: 2 TO 4

Freshly squeezed blood-orange juice is recommended for the marinade, but regular orange juice can be substituted if necessary.

About ½ cup freshly squeezed
  blood-orange juice, from 1½ sweet
  oranges, the remaining ½ orange
  thinly sliced and reserved
3 tablespoons prepared ginger
  tamari sauce
2 tablespoons port
2 cloves garlic, minced
½ teaspoon sea salt
½ to 1 teaspoon Szechuan peppercorns
4 chicken thighs
A few sprigs of fresh cilantro

Mix together the orange juice, tamari sauce, port, garlic, salt, and peppercorns in a bowl. Pierce the chicken thighs with a fork a few times on each side, and arrange them in a shallow nonreactive baking dish. Pour the marinade over the thighs, coating them thoroughly, and marinate for 2 to 3 hours in the refrigerator. Remove from the refrigerator 20 minutes before proceeding.

Preheat the broiler to high.

Transfer the thighs to a broiling pan lined with aluminum foil and cook for 20 to 25 minutes or until done (see page 162), basting and turning once during cooking.

Garnish each piece with a slice or two of the reserved orange and sprigs of cilantro.

Suggested Wine: Full-bodied red, such as a Rioja or California Cabernet Sauvignon

Fragrant spices and herbs are set out on fabric printed with a detailed farmyard scene.

FOLLOWING PAGES: *A rustic country table set for a buffet lunch features many new and antique ornamental chickens, including china or earthenware nesting hens, funky rooster-patterned glasses, wooden hen and cock napkin rings, miniature hen figurines, and a candy container shaped like a chick (its head serves as the lid).*

Lemon-Mint Barbecued Chicken & Onion Brochettes

SERVINGS: 4

When we planted our new herb garden we forgot how prolific mint is, though we are happy to find uses for the abundance of different varieties grown. Traditional drinks and dishes of Middle Eastern origin frequently incorporate lemon and mint, and it is a classic combination for outdoor grilling of meats and poultry that we enjoy all summer long. A favorite accompaniment for this dish, also of Middle Eastern as well as Mediterranean origins, is a sauté of drained canned chickpeas cooked in olive oil, finely minced garlic, and fresh parsley.

This recipe, like the other outdoor grilling recipes in this chapter, is prepared on a gas grill, which is slower than charcoal. I most often use disposable bamboo skewers, in 8- or 10-inch lengths, serving two per person. They should be soaked in water beforehand to prevent them from burning during grilling.

Juice of 2 large lemons

1 tablespoon olive oil

3 tablespoons finely chopped fresh mint

1 teaspoon sugar

1 clove elephant garlic, chopped

½ teaspoon sea salt

1¼ to 1½ pounds boneless, skinless chicken breasts, cut into 1½-inch chunks

16 small white onions (about 2 inches by 1 inch), peeled

8 bamboo skewers, soaked in water

Mix the lemon juice, olive oil, mint, sugar, garlic, and salt together in a non-reactive baking dish. Toss the chicken chunks in the marinade until thoroughly coated; set aside in the refrigerator for at least 30 minutes or up to 1 hour. Remove the chicken from the refrigerator about 20 minutes before the final preparation.

While the chicken is marinating, bring a saucepan of salted water with the onions to a boil and cook for 10 minutes; drain and set aside.

Thread the onions and chicken chunks onto the skewers.

Preheat the gas grill to high.

Place the brochettes on the grill and cook for 5 minutes over high heat, turning them over once. Lower the temperature to medium and cook for 7 to 8 minutes or until done (see page 162), turning the brochettes once or twice more during the cooking.

Suggested Beverage: Sugared spearmint tea or a Moroccan red wine, such as Boulaoune

Mustard-Chive Brochettes

SERVINGS: 4

This recipe, like the other outdoor grilling recipes in this chapter, is prepared on a gas grill, which is a slower grilling method than charcoal. I most often use disposable bamboo skewers, in 8- or 10-inch lengths, serving two per person. They should be soaked in water beforehand to prevent them from burning during grilling.

4 tablespoons Dijon mustard

⅔ cup heavy cream

2 tablespoons chopped fresh chives

Sea salt

Freshly ground pepper

1¼ to 1½ pounds boneless, skinless chicken breasts, cut into 1½-inch chunks

12 new potatoes, 1 to 1½ inches in diameter (or larger potatoes cut in half)

Paprika

8 bamboo skewers, soaked in water

Mix together the mustard, cream, and chives, and salt and pepper to taste; remove and reserve 3 tablespoons of this marinade.

Arrange the chicken chunks in one layer in a shallow nonreactive baking dish. Pour the marinade over the chicken, turn to coat, and marinate for 2 to 3 hours in the refrigerator.

While the chicken is marinating, bring a large pot of water to a boil, add some salt, and boil the potatoes until almost—but not quite—tender, 10 to 15 minutes. Drain thoroughly and season with salt, pepper, and paprika.

Thread the chicken pieces and potatoes onto the skewers.

Preheat the gas grill to high.

Place the brochettes on the grill and cook for 5 minutes over high heat, turning them over once. Lower the temperature to medium and cook for 7 to 8 minutes or until done (see page 162), turning the brochettes once or twice more during the cooking. Drizzle with the reserved sauce and serve.

Suggested Wine: Red such as Chiroubles

For the chicken collector, milk glass offers a great variety of desirable objects. Covered dishes and statuettes from the late nineteenth century were extremely popular in rooster, hen, chick, and egg forms. Many survive as originals or reproductions, as the original patented molds often out-lived the glass factory, were passed on, and continued in use.

This blue-headed nesting hen, featuring the combination of plain white and color incorporated in the glass, was produced by or from one of the molds of the Westmoreland Glass Company in Grapeville, Pennsylvania (1890–1985), which manufactured some of the finest quality milk glass in America.

OPPOSITE: Another milk-glass dish features a chick emerging from the center of a pile of eggs as its cover and a bottom finished with a lacy edge. This piece shows the mark of the Atterbury factory, also in Pennsylvania, and the piece's patent date of August 6, 1889. The Atterbury name is another highly desirable mark for collections.

Soy-Ginger Grilled Brochettes

SERVINGS: 4

*T*his dish is nicely flavored by a marinade that incorporates traditional Asian ingredients. It is prepared on a gas grill, which is slower than charcoal. I most often use disposable bamboo skewers, in 8- or 10-inch lengths, serving two per person. The skewers should be soaked in water beforehand to prevent them from burning.

6 tablespoons soy sauce

6 tablespoons sake

1 clove elephant garlic, chopped

2 tablespoons plus 1 teaspoon chopped fresh ginger

1 teaspoon brown sugar

3 scallions, finely chopped

¼ teaspoon sea salt

Freshly ground pepper

1½ pounds boneless, skinless chicken breasts, cut into 1½-inch chunks

¾ pound broccoli florets

⅔ cup tiny pearl onions

Peanut oil

8 bamboo skewers, soaked in water

Mix together the soy sauce, sake, garlic, ginger, brown sugar, scallions, salt, and pepper to taste.

Arrange the chicken pieces in one layer in a shallow nonreactive baking dish. Pour the marinade over the chicken, turn to coat thoroughly, and marinate for 2 to 3 hours in the refrigerator.

While the chicken is marinating, blanch the broccoli in boiling water for 2 to 3 minutes until barely tender; drain. Blanch the pearl onions for 3 minutes until almost tender; drain and peel them. Drizzle the vegetables lightly with oil. Remove the chicken from the refrigerator 20 minutes before proceeding.

Preheat the gas grill to high.

Thread the chicken pieces and vegetables onto the skewers.

Place the brochettes on the grill and cook for 5 minutes over high heat, turning them over once. Lower the temperature to medium and cook for 7 to 8 minutes or until done (see page 162), turning the brochettes once or twice more during the cooking.

Suggested Wine: Dry rosé from Bordeaux

*C*hicken designs for items for the cook, the kitchen, or the collector, hold a popular position in home furnishings.

Chicken-topped metal skewers for the barbecue chef who has everything and the collector who can't have enough, iron cocks and hen handles and knobs are perfect for the chicken lover's kitchen cabinets and drawers.

Sugar & Spice Grilled Brochettes with Plums & Sweet Onions

SERVINGS: 4

An Italian ceramic rooster bowl, created by a contemporary potter, is shaped and colorfully handpainted in an abstract style.

Nectarines can be substituted for the plums in this recipe, which is prepared outdoors on a gas grill. Use disposable bamboo skewers, in 8- to 10-inch lengths (two per person), soaked in water beforehand to prevent them from burning.

1 tablespoon *each of finely chopped fresh sage, rosemary, and marjoram*

1 teaspoon *sea salt*

2 teaspoons *sugar*

½ teaspoon *paprika*

Pinch of cayenne

1½ *pounds boneless, skinless chicken breasts, cut into 1½-inch chunks*

Juice of 1 lime

2 *tablespoons honey*

1 *teaspoon Dijon mustard*

Sea salt

Freshly ground pepper

4 *large plums, pitted and quartered*

3 *large red onions, peeled and cut into 6 wedges each*

8 *bamboo skewers, soaked in water*

Mix together the herbs, salt, sugar, paprika, and cayenne in a large bowl; toss the chicken pieces in the mixture. Let the chicken stand for 30 minutes.

Mix together the lime juice, honey, mustard, and salt and pepper to taste in a bowl. Place the plums in a shallow dish and pour the mixture over, turning to coat each piece thoroughly. Let stand, turning and basting a few times.

Meanwhile, thread the onion sections on some of the skewers.

After the chicken and fruit have marinated, make up skewers of the chicken alternating with the plum pieces.

Preheat the gas grill to high.

When the grill is ready, cook the onion skewers for 8 minutes, turning them twice. Place the chicken and fruit skewers on the grill and cook for 5 minutes, turning them once. Lower the temperature to medium and cook for an additional 7 to 8 minutes or until done (see page 162), turning the onion and chicken skewers once or twice during the cooking.

Suggested Wine: Red Beaujolais, such as Moulin-à-Vent

Lime-Ginger Satay

SERVINGS: 4 TO 6

This recipe, and the other outdoor grilling recipes in this chapter, is prepared on a gas grill, which is a slower grilling method than charcoal. The sauce is common in Indonesian and Thai dishes. Any Asian-style noodles are a nice accompaniment, topped with more of the same sauce.

5 tablespoons soy sauce

2 tablespoons prepared fish sauce

4 tablespoons freshly squeezed lime juice

5 cloves garlic, 2 chopped, 3 minced

1 tablespoon chopped fresh ginger

2 whole chicken breasts, boned and skinned, cut into long strips

2 teaspoons peanut oil

1 tablespoon plus 1 teaspoon green chile sauce (medium hot)

2 tablespoons prepared hoisin sauce

⅔ cup broth or stock

3 tablespoons creamy peanut butter

½ teaspoon brown sugar

Bamboo skewers, soaked in water

Combine the soy sauce, fish sauce, lime juice, chopped garlic, and ginger in a bowl.

Place the chicken strips in a nonreactive shallow dish and pour the mixture over. Let the chicken stand for 30 minutes.

Meanwhile, heat the oil over low heat in a small saucepan; add the minced garlic and cook, stirring, for 2 to 3 minutes. Add the chile and hoisin sauces, chicken broth, peanut butter, and brown sugar to the pan, stirring constantly. Remove the pan from the heat and blend thoroughly with a spoon. Pour the sauce into a pitcher or sauce boat and set aside.

Preheat the gas grill to high.

Drain the chicken strips of the excess marinade; discard the marinade.

Thread the chicken onto the skewers. Place them on the grill and cook for 5 minutes over high heat, turning them over once. Lower the temperature to medium and cook for 7 to 8 minutes or until done (see page 162), turning the satays once or twice more during the cooking.

Pass the peanut sauce at the table.

Suggested Wine: Chablis

A pair of porcelain glaze roosters are thought to be nineteenth century, dating from the late Qing Dynasty period (1644 to the early twentieth century). This was a period during which the ceramic industry benefited from renewed imperial support and contact with Western art and technology. The intense blue-green bodies are incised for detailing and make an interesting contrast with the aubergine used for the cocks' combs, wattles and bases. While the design has an Asian manner, the ceramic pair was made for export to Western markets.

Pan-Grilled Cilantro Chicken Burgers

SERVINGS: 4

Serve these burgers, an adaptation of the great American hamburger, with the usual buns, relishes, fries, chips, salads, corn on the cob, and so on. Or give the dish a Southwestern focus as I've done here, and serve with a selection of salsas, nachos and cheese, or tortillas.

Keep in mind that chicken burgers, like any other chicken dish, must be thoroughly cooked. The recipe uses a heavy ridged grill pan on top of the stove.

½ pound ground chicken
½ pound ground turkey
½ pound ground pork
2 tablespoons finely chopped cilantro
3 teaspoons jalapeño sauce
½ teaspoon sea salt (or to preference)
2 to 3 grindings of freshly ground pepper
Corn oil

Suggested Wine: Chilled Provençal rosé, such as Bandol

Mix the chicken, turkey, and pork together in a bowl with the cilantro and jalapeño sauce. Season with salt and pepper.

Shape the mixture into 4 burgers; they will be about 6 ounces each.

Spray or brush the grill pan with corn oil and heat the pan, gradually increasing the temperature until its surface is very hot. Place the burgers on the pan and cook for about 8 minutes each side or until cooked through (see page 162).

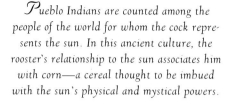

Pueblo Indians are counted among the people of the world for whom the cock represents the sun. In this ancient culture, the rooster's relationship to the sun associates him with corn—a cereal thought to be imbued with the sun's physical and mystical powers.

The Pueblo were known to use corn in rituals of divination as other cultures used the pecking and scratching patterns of the chicken to read the future.

OPPOSITE: A hen centerpiece is covered in seed corn and detailed with beak, cock's comb, and wings made of tin.

BELOW: This clay planter in a primitive style is from Mexico. Planters like this one are popular in gardens throughout the Southwestern United States.

3

SAUTÉ
& FRY

IT IS UNFORTUNATE THAT FRIED FOOD SOMETIMES conjures up negative associations and is written off by many as unappetizing and unhealthful. Too many "greasy spoon" and fast-food eating establishments have contributed to this image, while the medical establishment has focused attention on the harmful effects of too much of certain kinds of fats in the diet. 'Tis a pity; some of the most delicious dishes are fried. And with today's non-stick cookware, knowledge of "good" fats versus "bad" fats, and the variety of cooking oils and oil sprays available, you can prepare enjoyable fried foods. As Julia Child recently suggested when discussing her views on special diets for health or weight loss—don't eliminate, just moderate and be sensible.

Frying cooks food fairly rapidly in hot fat over moderate to high heat. Differences among frying techniques can generally be said to rest on how much fat is used in the cooking. Pan-frying uses little fat, perhaps as little as a coating for the bottom of the pan or as much as a depth of ½ inch. Deep-frying submerges the food

pieces in the fat completely. Sauté and stir-fry are two other methods of cooking in fat.

Sauté comes from the French *sauter*, meaning "to jump" to describe the way food moves with the shaking of the pan to keep it from burning and sticking in very hot fat. Sauté refers to both a process that finishes the cooking of food as well as browning ingredients of a dish in preparation for further cooking by a different method, such as stewing. As a finished dish, a sauté often includes vegetables and involves adding liquid at the end to create a sauce for the dish. In stir-frying, small or bite-sized pieces of meat and vegetable cook very rapidly in a minimum of fat, usually in a wok, where the food is briskly stirred.

It is automatic to think of stir-frying as the definitive method of Chinese cooking. However, this method seems to have developed much later than others out of practical and economical needs rather than culinary experiment.

The farming methods of the last two centuries of the

A French copperplate engraving, probably from a nineteenth-century French journal, depicts a barnyard scene replete with roosters, hens, and chicks. It stands framed next to a white porcelain hen from the 1950s.

Han period (202 B.C.–A.D. 220) required workers to leave their villages and live in the fields from the early spring through harvest time in the autumn. A mobile and quick method of cooking that would maximize the peasant's work time and minimize fuel consumption to prepare meals was needed. It is thought that stir-frying evolved as the solution. The assumption that this method developed with the peasants rather than the privileged would explain why there are no written accounts and why a sure knowledge of the use of stir-frying dates only from the Tang era (618–907).

In this chapter a variety of frying methods are used for a variety of cuts of chicken. The seasoned bread-crumb and batter coatings not only carry various flavors, but protect the meat by creating a seal that keeps the inside juicy and the exterior crisp. Dry spice rubs provide a good way to get great flavor while minimizing the "fat factor" by utilizing the quickest-cooking parts, little oil and fast cooking.

Here are some recommendations for successful frying:

❤ Use a fine mesh spatter cover to protect yourself from burns or stains and to keep the kitchen clean.

❤ Turn pan handles away from you to prevent dangerous and messy spills.

❤ Cook in fats with high smoke point (see page 163).

❤ Do not crowd the chicken—use pans roomy enough or fry in two batches.

❤ When deep-frying, fill the pot no more than half way to allow for the expansion of the fat as it heats.

❤ Use a frying or candy thermometer.

*Chicken Smothered
in Eight Onions*

Sage & Beaufort Cheese Cutlets

*Breaded Chicken Cutlets with
Chopped Tomatoes & Arugula*

*Chicken Cutlets with
Wild Mushrooms in Cream Sauce*

*Saffron Chicken Thighs
with Lime Sauce*

*Breaded Chicken Cutlets
with Fried Green Tomatoes*

*Chicken Legs with Tomatoes
& Black Olives*

*Chicken Thighs & Carrots
in Orange Cream Sauce*

Southern Fried Chicken

*Cornmeal-Battered
Chicken Livers*

*Paprika Chicken Cutlets
with Baked Sauerkraut*

*Peppery Chicken Patties
with Pepper Cream*

*Chicken Cutlets
with Lemon & Capers*

Sesame Chicken Fingers

Chicken Fondue, Bourguignonne Style

Chicken Smothered in Eight Onions

SERVINGS: 4

*T*his is adapted from my mother's recipe for liver or steak with slowly cooked onions, which often turned up on our dinner table.

1 tablespoon olive oil

2 whole chicken breasts, boned and skinned, halved and pounded into ⅜-inch-thick pieces (4 pieces)

Sea salt

Freshly ground pepper

½ teaspoon dried thyme

2 tablespoons unsalted butter

2 cloves garlic, finely chopped

1 large red onion, cut into ¼-inch slices

1 large Vidalia onion, or other variety of sweet onion, cut into ¼-inch slices

1 large white onion, cut into ¼-inch slices

6 scallions, including most of their greens, cut into 1-inch pieces

2 medium leeks, white and pale green parts only, sliced into 1-inch rounds and washed carefully

2 large shallots, sliced into rounds

½ cup dry white wine

⅔ cup chicken broth or stock

2 tablespoons flour

⅓ cup chopped fresh chives

Heat the oil in a sauté pan. Add the chicken pieces and brown on both sides, about 4 minutes per side. Remove from the pan, season with salt, pepper, and the thyme, and set aside on a warmed dish. Cover the chicken loosely with foil and keep warm.

Wipe the pan clean. Add the butter to the pan over medium heat. When it has just started to foam, add the garlic and cook for 1 minute. Then add all the onions, leeks, and shallots and gently cook until the onions are translucent and softened but not browned, 8 to 10 minutes.

Add the wine to the onions and cook over high heat until the liquid has evaporated. Add the chicken broth,

bring to a boil, and cook until the liquid is reduced by half, 8 to 10 minutes.

Lower the heat. Sprinkle the flour over the onions and mix thoroughly.

Add the chicken pieces to the onions and cook for 3 minutes over medium heat, or until done (see page 162). Stir in the chives and cook for a minute longer.

Transfer the chicken to a serving platter and pour the onions and pan drippings over.

Suggested Wine: Spanish or Chilean red wine, such as Rioja

OPPOSITE: *Straight from the market, various types of onions and their cousins lay on a kitchen towel printed with a rooster silhouette. Nearby, a painted iron rooster doorstop functions as a bookend.*

RIGHT: *The hen with chicks and the rooster are cast-iron doorstops in a nineteenth century folk-art style.*

Sage & Beaufort Cheese Cutlets

SERVINGS: 4

*B*eaufort is an excellent, full-bodied cheese from the Savoie region of France. It has terrific melting capacity and is worth looking for. However, Comté or Emmental cheese can be substituted.

2 tablespoons chopped fresh sage leaves, or 2 teaspoons dried sage

⅔ cup dry focaccia bread crumbs, or other herbed bread crumbs (see Note, page 34)

⅔ cup shredded Beaufort cheese, or Comté or Emmental cheese

2 chicken breasts, boned, skinned, halved, and pounded into ¼-inch-thick cutlets (4 pieces)

Flour

1 egg, lightly beaten

2 tablespoons vegetable oil

Mix the chopped sage with the bread crumbs and the cheese.

Dredge the chicken cutlets in the flour, then dip into the egg, letting the excess drop off. Coat the pieces thoroughly with the bread-crumb mixture.

Heat the oil in a skillet or sauté pan over medium heat.

Fry the cutlets in the oil until the coating is golden brown and crisp and the chicken is done (see page 162), 3 to 4 minutes per side.

Suggested Wine: Light red burgundy such as Chiroubles or Saint-Amour, slightly chilled

Breaded Chicken Cutlets with Chopped Tomatoes & Arugula

SERVINGS: 6

This is a variation on the classic Milanese veal dish that can be found on restaurant menus and, because it is as quick and easy as it is delicious, in private homes. The veal cutlet is breaded and fried, then topped with a chopped "salad" of tomatoes and sometimes greens. It is served just warm or at room temperature. Oil and vinegar are placed at the table and each guest dresses the dish to his taste.

In my version, chicken breasts replace the veal, and the dish is topped with a generous salad of chopped arugula and tomatoes. Along with the oil and vinegar, I usually place a chunk of Parmigiano-Reggiano or pecorino cheese and a cheese shaver on the table for those who desire additional flavor.

Dredge the chicken cutlets in the flour, then dip into the egg, letting the excess drop off. Coat the pieces thoroughly with the bread crumbs.

Heat half of the oil in a heavy skillet that will hold three cutlets comfortably. When the oil is hot enough to sizzle, add the first batch of cutlets and fry them until the coating is evenly golden brown and the chicken is done (see page 162), 2 to 3 minutes on each side. Adjust the heat as necessary. Set the cutlets aside. Add the remaining oil to the skillet and repeat the process with the remaining cutlets.

Arrange the chicken on individual serving plates. Divide the arugula and tomatoes over the cutlets. Pass the olive oil, vinegar, basil, and cheese at the table.

Suggested Wine: A good Soave

- 3 chicken breasts, boned, skinned, halved, and pounded into ¼-inch-thick cutlets (6 pieces)
- Flour
- 2 eggs, lightly beaten
- 1 to 1⅓ cups focaccia bread crumbs or other herbed bread crumbs (see Note, page 34)
- 4 tablespoons olive oil, plus additional for serving
- 6 medium vine-ripened tomatoes, cut into large dice
- ¾ pound arugula, coarsely chopped
- White wine vinegar
- 6 tablespoons finely chopped fresh basil (optional)
- Wedge of Parmigiano-Reggiano or pecorino cheese (optional)

Breaded Chicken Cutlets with Chopped Tomatoes and Arugula are served on rooster-patterned plates. Tiny porcelain knicknacks provide additional decoration. With its floral rooster-and-hen border, the tablecloth reproduces the look of classic chintz patterns.

Chicken Cutlets with Wild Mushrooms in Cream Sauce

SERVINGS: 4

*T*he combination of chicken, mushrooms, and cream with a flavoring of Madeira or Marsala wine is a quite classic one. Perhaps the best-known version of all is the French dish *suprême de volaille*. Here the mushrooms are more prominent, to intensify the flavor of the dish.

A mixture of dried and fresh morels is ideal, but fresh morels are not always available—and they're expensive when they are. Excellent substitutes are chanterelles, shiitake tops, or cremini mushrooms. I often just increase the quantity of dried morels, though, as I prefer their very distinctive flavor. Serve with wild or white rice, or risotto to optimize the enjoyment of the sauce.

1½ ounces dried morels (or 6 ounces if using dried only)

¼ cup plus 1 tablespoon Marsala or Madeira (2 tablespoons if using only dried mushrooms)

1 to 2 tablespoons vegetable oil

2 whole chicken breasts, boned, skinned, halved, and lightly pounded into ½-inch-thick cutlets (4 pieces)

Sea salt

Freshly ground white pepper

4 tablespoons unsalted butter

3 tablespoons plus 1 teaspoon finely chopped shallots

5 ounces fresh morels (or chanterelles, shiitake tops, or cremini), cut into ¼-inch slices

¼ cup beef broth or stock

1 cup plus 2 tablespoons crème fraîche or sour cream

Wash the dried morels, then place them in a small bowl. Add the 1 tablespoon wine and water to almost cover, and soak for 40 minutes to reconstitute. Drain the mushrooms, reserving the liquid.

Heat the oil in a sauté pan. Add the cutlets, and cook until the outside is lightly browned and the chicken is done (see page 162), 3 to 4 minutes on each side. Remove from the pan, season with salt and pepper, and keep warm.

Wipe the pan clean. Melt the butter in the pan over medium-high heat, add the shallots, and sweat them for 1 to 2 minutes. Add the soaked mushrooms and ¼ cup of the reserved liquid, and cook over high heat for 2 to 3 minutes to evaporate the liquid. Lower the heat to medium-high and add the fresh mushrooms. Cook for 2 to 3 minutes, stirring.

Add the stock and the ¼ cup wine, bring to boil, and cook until the liquid is reduced by half. Stir in the crème fraîche and immediately lower the heat and cook for 2 to 3 minutes; do not boil. Add the chicken, spooning the sauce over, and heat through.

Place the chicken on a serving platter and pour the sauce over.

Suggested Wine: Meursault

Saffron Chicken Thighs with Lime Sauce

*C*hef Bernard Collier of the Parisian restaurant Les Potiers made a similar dish with beef fillets. I saw the recipe in French *Elle* and adapted it for chicken. Serve with sautéed leeks and asparagus.

8 chicken thighs, skinned and boned
2 teaspoons saffron threads, crumbled
Sea salt
Freshly ground pepper
Flour
2 tablespoons olive oil
¾ cup dry white wine
Juice of 3 small limes
1 tablespoon grated lime zest
½ cup crème fraîche or sour cream
10 to 12 green peppercorns in brine, rinsed and drained

Sprinkle the chicken with half the saffron, season with salt and pepper, and dredge each piece lightly in flour.

Heat the olive oil in a sauté pan over medium-high heat, add the thighs, and cook for 7 to 8 minutes on each side or until done (see page 162). Transfer the chicken to a heated serving dish and keep warm.

Return the pan to the heat, pour in the wine, and scrape up any browned bits. Add the lime juice and zest and the remaining saffron to the pan and cook over high heat until the liquid is almost completely reduced.

Add the crème fraîche and bring the mixture just to a boil; immediately lower the heat and add the peppercorns. Stir for a minute or two and then remove from the heat. Pour the sauce over the chicken and serve.

Suggested Wine: White Bordeaux Graves

*T*oday this mold hangs as a decorative plaque in a kitchen along with other figurative molds in copper, tin, and iron. But in its day the large handsome design, carved out of wood and with intricate ornamental detail, might have made beautiful gingerbread roosters.

Breaded Chicken Cutlets with Fried Green Tomatoes

SERVINGS: 6

This is an all-American version of coated cutlets, of which the possibilities seem to be endless.

6 to 8 tablespoons olive oil

½ teaspoon hot red pepper sauce or jalapeño chile sauce

Sea salt

Freshly ground pepper

3 large green tomatoes, cut into large dice

1⅓ cups cornbread crumbs mixed with ½ teaspoon hot red pepper flakes

3 chicken breasts, boned, skinned, halved, and pounded into ¼-inch-thick cutlets (6 pieces)

Flour

2 eggs, lightly beaten

Combine 2 tablespoons of the oil, the hot sauce, and salt and pepper to taste in a mixing bowl. Add the tomatoes and toss to coat them thoroughly. Add 3 tablespoons of the cornbread-crumb mixture and toss again.

Heat a nonstick wok or sauté pan, add the tomatoes, and cook until tender, 5 to 10 minutes. Set aside and keep warm.

Dredge 3 of the chicken cutlets in the flour, then dip them into the eggs, letting the excess drop off. Coat the cutlets with some of the remaining cornbread-crumb mixture.

Heat 2 tablespoons of the oil in a large skillet. When the oil sizzles, fry the first batch of cutlets in the pan for 2 to 3 minutes per side until cooked through (see page 162) and golden. Set the cutlets aside and keep them warm while you repeat the process with the remaining cutlets, adding oil as needed.

Arrange the chicken among individual serving plates, and top with the fried tomatoes.

Suggested Wine: Dry white California, such as Chardonnay

OPPOSITE: *Decorated tea towels—some homemade—hang from a Shaker towel rail in a country kitchen and display a range of charm, from sweet to elegant.*

BELOW: *Old engraved images that find their way into the public domain may appear—and reappear—on contemporary pieces. Here, an antique fancy breed cock is reduced as a one-color outline design for a plate from a currently produced breakfast service.*

Chicken Legs with Tomatoes & Black Olives

SERVINGS: 4

*P*rovençal or Niçoise? That is the ongoing question *chez famille Arnaud!*

Polenta has been a favorite dish of my husband since childhood; day-old polenta, grilled and topped with prepared eggplant caviar or artichoke tapenade as a spread and served with this Mediterranean-style dish, brings back fond memories. Fresh oregano is the distinctive note here, but fresh thyme can be substituted.

2 tablespoons vegetable oil

4 large chicken legs (about 6 ounces each)

½ cup olive oil

1½ pounds fresh tomatoes, peeled, seeded and diced (or about 14 ounces canned tomatoes, diced and drained)

8 cloves garlic, crushed through a garlic press

1 tablespoon fresh oregano leaves

Sea salt

Freshly ground pepper

6 ounces oil-cured black olives, pitted

Hot red pepper flakes

½ pound ripe cherry tomatoes

Heat the vegetable oil in a sauté pan. Add the chicken and brown, starting with the skin side down, for about 8 minutes total. Remove the chicken and set aside.

Add the olive oil to the pan, then the tomatoes, and cook over high heat for 5 minutes. Stir in the garlic and oregano, and season with salt and pepper. Return the chicken legs to the pan. Cover, lower the heat to medium, and cook for 20 to 25 minutes or until the chicken is done (see page 162).

Sprinkle the olives with the hot red pepper flakes. Add the olives and cherry tomatoes to the chicken and cook for 5 minutes, or until the tomatoes have just split open.

Arrange the chicken legs in a serving dish and top with the sauce.

Suggested Wine: Lightly chilled red Côte de Provence

LEFT: *A hauty cock decorates Italian egg dishes from the 1930s, in hues typical of ceramic objects and tiles of the Mediterranean region.*

OPPOSITE: *A somewhat stylized version of a rooster decorates a contemporary Italian oil jug. The jug's ancient shape helps pour liquid in a slow and steady stream. Clearly, these designs have prevailing appeal.*

Chicken Thighs & Carrots in Orange Cream Sauce

SERVINGS: 4

4 large chicken thighs
(about 6 ounces each)

Sea salt

Freshly ground pepper

2 tablespoons vegetable oil

5 tablespoons finely chopped shallots

¾ cup chicken broth or stock

¾ cup dry white wine

1 teaspoon fresh thyme leaves

1 pound carrots, scraped and cut into
¼- by 2-inch matchsticks (4 cups)

Juice of 2 blood oranges or the sweetest
other variety available

¼ cup cognac

2 tablespoons grated orange zest

½ cup crème fraîche or sour cream

Chopped flat-leaf parsley

Season the chicken with salt and pepper.

Heat the oil in a large skillet or sauté pan over medium heat; place the chicken in the pan top side down and brown the chicken to a light golden color, turning once or twice. Remove the chicken from the pan.

Add the shallots to the pan and cook until translucent.

Add the broth, wine, and thyme, and bring the mixture to a boil. Cook until the liquid is reduced by one-third.

Return the chicken, top side down, to the skillet, and cook, covered, for 10 to 15 minutes.

Turn the chicken pieces over and add the carrots and orange juice. Stir and toss, cover, and cook for 10 to 15 minutes more or until the thighs are done (see page 162) and the carrots are tender but still crisp.

With a slotted spoon remove the chicken and carrots from the skillet and transfer them to a heated serving dish and keep warm.

Heat the cognac in a saucepan, then pour it into the sauce in the pan; ignite it and, when the flames subside, add the orange zest and bring just to a boil.

Reduce the heat to low and add the crème fraîche. Cook, without boiling, for 3 minutes; pour over the chicken and carrots, sprinkle with the parsley, and serve.

Suggested Wine: Full-bodied white, such as Meursault or Chablis

Arts and crafts seem to favor rooster or cock images over the hen. And it is equally true that the male bird is the more dominant in religion, literature, culture, and custom. Nesting hens and hens with their eggs, chicks, or the rooster are the most common views presented; she is most often associated with benevolent qualities like nurturing and patience.

As a symbol of fussy mothering care, the term "mother hen" is used for a person who is overbearing and nearly smothering in her— or his—attentiveness.

OPPOSITE: *The docility and sweet nature implied by the nesting position is captured in a large contemporary charcoal line drawing by a New York designer and in a plump painted ceramic figure by an English potter. A standing hen made of raffia that is perched to the side in the dining room is from the Philippines.*

Southern Fried Chicken

SERVINGS: 4 TO 6

The great American classic may have its roots—or at least the roots of its fame—in the South, but the dish is in fact enjoyed from coast to coast and border to border. Even in a Yankee household like mine, Southern fried chicken was considered a treat. My mother served it hot on Sunday or cold for picnics at the beach. She claimed that her version's perfection was due to four crucial elements: dipping the chicken in buttermilk, coating it one piece at a time by shaking it in a brown paper bag, frying in reserved bacon drippings and Crisco, and using a heavy cast-iron pan she pampered as if it were a pet.

Finish the meal off with all-American specialties like grits or hush puppies, corn on the cob, tomatoes, and an apple or peach pie for dessert.

Here is one method for fried chicken, with three different herb-spice combinations to apply to three different parts of the chicken. Of course, the formulas are interchangeable, and you should feel free to apply the coatings suggested for one part to another.

For fried thighs

- 3 tablespoons dried thyme
- 1 tablespoon dried oregano
- 1 tablespoon granulated garlic
- 1 tablespoon onion powder
- 1 teaspoon salt
- ½ teaspoon freshly ground pepper
- 8 chicken thighs
- ½ cup cornmeal
- 1 egg, lightly beaten
- ½ cup buttermilk
- ½ cup flour
- Vegetable shortening

For fried legs

- 3 tablespoons dried rosemary leaves, crumbled
- 2 tablespoons granulated garlic
- 1 teaspoon sea salt
- ½ teaspoon freshly ground pepper
- 6 to 8 chicken drumsticks
- 1 egg, lightly beaten
- ½ cup buttermilk
- 1 cup flour
- Vegetable shortening

For fried breast nuggets

- 3 tablespoons herbes de Provence
- 1 teaspoon dried lavender buds
- 1 teaspoon onion powder
- 2 teaspoons granulated garlic
- 1 teaspoon salt
- ½ teaspoon freshly ground pepper
- 2 whole chicken breasts, boned, skinned, and cut into 1- by 2-inch nuggets
- 1 egg, lightly beaten
- ½ cup milk
- 1 cup flour
- Vegetable shortening

A ceramic chicken bottle stopper from Portugal tops a German bottle showing a country scene in relief.

Mix the dried herbs and spices together in a bowl. Reserve 1 teaspoon for the egg mixture and 1 tablespoon for the flour mixture.

Rub the remaining seasoning mixture on the chicken pieces, under and on top of the skin (see Note, page 6). Place the pieces in a dish, cover, and refrigerate for 2 hours or overnight. Bring the chicken to room temperature when you are ready to continue.

Combine the egg, milk or buttermilk, and 1 teaspoon of the reserved seasoning mixture in another bowl.

Combine the flour or flour-and-cornmeal mixture with 1 tablespoon of the reserved seasoning mixture in a bowl. Set aside.

Melt the vegetable shortening in a deep, heavy cast-iron or enameled pan or electric fryer; it should yield enough oil in which to submerge the pieces. The oil should reach a temperature of 350 degrees on a fry or candy thermometer.

Dredge the chicken pieces, a few at a time, in the egg mixture, letting the excess drop off, then dredge in the flour mixture. Shake off the excess flour.

Immediately fry the chicken pieces in the oil a few at a time, about 25 minutes for dark meat on the bone, 20 minutes for breasts with bone, and 15 minutes for the boneless breast nuggets. They should be golden and cooked through (see page 162).

Suggested Beverage: Ice Tea! Beer! Or, in a pinch, white wine, such as St. Vérans

Cornmeal-Battered Chicken Livers

SERVINGS: 4

I tasted a dish of batter-fried chicken livers as an appetizer at Georgia Brown's, a restaurant specializing in Southern cooking in Washington, D.C., and loved it. At home, I re-created it as a main dish. Served on a bed of flavorful collard greens with corn-battered fried green tomatoes, it's a hearty meal.

1½ pounds chicken livers
½ teaspoon sea salt
Freshly ground pepper
¼ teaspoon cayenne
1 tablespoon granulated garlic
Cornmeal flour
2 eggs, beaten
Vegetable oil

Season the livers with the salt and pepper.

Combine the cayenne, garlic, and cornmeal flour.

Heat the oil in a sauté pan over medium-high heat.

Lightly flour the livers, dip them in the eggs, shaking off the excess, and roll them in the flour again. Shake off any excess flour. When the oil is hot, add the livers and fry them, turning several times, until golden, 5 minutes or cooked through. Remove from the pan and serve.

Suggested Beverage: Beer or Sauvignon Blanc from California

Cornmeal-Battered Fried Green Tomatoes

2 cups cornmeal flour
Sea salt
Freshly ground pepper
Vegetable oil
2 to 3 large green tomatoes, or not very ripe red tomatoes, cut into ¼-inch slices
1 egg, beaten

Combine the flour with the salt and pepper to taste.

Pour oil into a heavy skillet to a depth of ¼ inch and heat. Dip the tomato slices in the flour mixture, then into the egg, shaking off the excess, then dip the slices into the flour again.

Fry the slices in the pan, turning once, for 3 to 5 minutes, or until golden on the outside and fork tender.

A picnic on a penthouse terrace provides
an opportunity to show off a wide range of
chicken artifacts. The setting may be urban
but the menu includes country favorites:
Southern Fried Chicken (see page 86),
Cornmeal-Battered Chicken Livers (see page 87),
a seasonal mixed tomato salad, and fresh corn
on the cob. The meal is served with a chilled
white wine specifically branded and labeled
for—and with—chicken.

FROM LEFT TO RIGHT: Contemporary tableware,
such as hand-painted glasses, a printed mat,
wooden salad servers, and a pottery bowl
highlight chickens in a variety of design styles
that vary from country rustic to sophisticated.

Today's market provides a wide selection
of rooster and hen statuary for the outdoors.
The cement chicken on the left is smartly
decorative left unpainted.

As a folk art subject, chickens are as popular
today as in ancient and "olden" times. Over
the centuries, and including today, artisans and
craftsmen have created these figures for use as
decorative or utilitarian objects, children's toys
and even religious emblems. In the basket are
a rooster assembled from a craft kit and an
eastern export hen; on the bench at far left is
a sitting hen of an eastern style and origin,
grouped on the table at right, a wooden folk art
rooster gobbles corn; a napkin holder and napkin
ring are fashioned as chickens.

Toward the center, hanging above the basket
of fried chicken, is a small-scale reproduction of
early American tin signage, originally designed
to advertise poultry and eggs.

To its right, a hen—called Helen by her
owners—is immortalized through taxidermy.
Evidently, once the pride of the coop, this hen
is now the prize of a collection.

Paprika Chicken Cutlets with Baked Sauerkraut

SERVINGS: 4

This recipe marries favorite dishes of both my husband's family and mine for sauerkraut with chicken. His French family simmers sauerkraut in wine and juniper berries on the stovetop to make traditional Alsatian dishes, while my Ukrainian family sautés or bakes sauerkraut with onions and salt pork as a vegetable dish. When Michel's uncle visited our house in London, he always prepared a choucroute with pork meats or with smoked and fresh fish. When my mother visited, she'd hold up her side and present a *kapusta* made with roast pork or kielbasa (which she purchased at a specialty butcher shop on New York City's Lower East Side and smuggled into England in her hand luggage).

Thus in our house, we make a chicken dish that can be executed with either kind of sauerkraut. Here, my mother's method for oven *kapusta* is the base.

¼ teaspoon freshly ground caraway seeds

4 tablespoons Dijon mustard

2 whole chicken breasts, boned, skinned, halved, and pounded to ¼-inch-thick cutlets, each pierced once or twice with a fork

3 tablespoons unsalted butter

4 ounces salt pork, cut into lardons (⅛- by 1-inch strips)

1 large onion, sliced to ¼-inch rounds and then quartered

2 pounds sauerkraut (bought loose from a shop or packaged in a bag or jar, not canned), drained, rinsed, and drained again

2 tablespoons sweet paprika, plus additional for cutlets

½ cup white wine

½ cup crème fraîche or sour cream

Sea salt

Freshly ground white pepper

Preheat the oven to 425 degrees.

Mix the caraway seeds into 3 tablespoons of the mustard. Brush the chicken cutlets with the mixture and marinate for 1 to 2 hours in the refrigerator. Bring the chicken back to room temperature before cooking.

Heat 2 tablespoons of the butter in an enameled cast-iron Dutch oven (or covered nonstick flame- and ovenproof pan) and sauté the salt pork over medium-high heat until the fatty part is transparent and starts to become golden.

Add the onion and cook until translucent and slightly soft but not browned. Lower the heat to medium. With a slotted spoon remove the onions and salt pork and set aside. Add the sauerkraut to the pot and cook just until it begins to brown, about 5 minutes.

Return the onions and salt pork to the pot and combine with the sauerkraut, cooking for an additional 3 minutes.

Sprinkle 2 tablespoons of the paprika into the sauerkraut and cook for 3 minutes.

Remove the pot from the heat, cover, and place it in the oven. Lower the temperature to 350 degrees, and bake for 15 minutes.

Uncover the pot and continue to bake for 10 to 15 minutes.

Meanwhile, heat the remaining 1 tablespoon of the butter in a sauté pan. Lightly sprinkle the cutlets with paprika and sauté them for 3 minutes on each side or until done (see page 162). Remove them from the pan to a serving dish and keep them warm.

Add the wine to the pan, scraping up the browned bits. Add the remaining 1 tablespoon of mustard and stir for 1 minute. Add the crème fraîche and cook, stirring, for 1 or 2 minutes to heat through; don't let the sauce boil. Season with salt and white pepper.

Serve the chicken on the sauerkraut and spoon the sauce over.

Suggested Wine: Dry white, such as Rully

The work of true folk artists exhibits characteristics particular to their communities and rarely reflects artistic developments beyond their borders. The objects these artists produce tend to be functional, impermanent and hand made. Design themes are drawn from the immediate world, and may be imbued with symbolic significance. Much of folk art is created with easily accessible natural materials like wood, tin, wax, straw, or paper.

OPPOSITE: *This free-standing wood carving depicting a young girl and her chickens in a barnyard coop was created by Antoni Kaminski, a member of the Polish Union of Folk Artists.*

ABOVE: *An almost heraldic design of symmetrical roosters surrounded by a geometric floral pattern is crafted from layers of colored paper. This modern cut-out from Poland represents a central European folk-art tradition that is still practiced today.*

Peppery Chicken Patties
with Pepper Cream

SERVINGS: 6 TO 8

This recipe was inspired by James McNair's Sautéed Chicken Cakes with Tomato and Sweet Pepper Sauce. In my variation, a combination of mildly hot poblano and sweet red bell and green Cubanelle peppers with just a bit of the hotter jalapeño balance to create a mild flavor. For a spicier dish, use more of the poblano and less of the sweet peppers, or add another half teaspoon of the jalapeños. My addition of cornbread crumbs and cilantro give this recipe a Southwestern accent. My sauce is a purée of sweet orange and yellow peppers with red onion blended into sour cream and served chilled.

4 tablespoons vegetable oil, plus
  additional as necessary
¼ cup minced Cubanelle peppers
  (frying peppers)
⅔ cup minced red bell peppers
⅓ cup minced poblano peppers
½ to 1 teaspoon minced
  jalapeño peppers
⅔ cup minced scallions
Sea salt
Freshly ground pepper
1½ pounds ground chicken
½ pound ground pork
2 cups cornbread crumbs
2 eggs, lightly beaten
½ cup heavy cream
¼ cup chopped fresh cilantro

1 tablespoon unsalted butter
1 cup chopped orange bell pepper
1 cup chopped yellow bell pepper
¾ cup chopped red onion
1 cup sour cream

Heat 2 tablespoons of the oil in a sauté pan. Add the peppers and scallions and cook until tender, without browning. Season with salt and pepper. Set the mixture aside to cool.

In a large mixing bowl, combine the chicken, pork, cornbread crumbs, eggs, and cream and blend thoroughly.

Add the pepper mixture to the chicken mixture; stir in the cilantro and combine thoroughly.

Line a baking sheet with aluminum foil. Shape the mixture into 8 patties and place them on the baking sheet. Put the sheet of patties in the refrigerator to set for 30 minutes.

While the patties are chilling, heat the butter in a nonstick sauté pan, add the orange and yellow peppers with the red onion, and cook until very tender; season with salt and pepper.

Transfer the pepper mixture to a food processor and blend to a paste. Set aside to cool.

Remove the patties from the refrigerator. Preheat the oven to 175 degrees. Heat 2 tablespoons of the oil in a sauté pan over medium-high heat. Fry a few patties at a time, without crowding them, for 4 to 5 minutes per side, or until cooked through; keep the finished patties warm on a baking dish in the oven until all are finished. Add more oil to the pan as needed.

When ready to serve, combine the sour cream with the pepper mixture and top each patty with a dollop.

Suggested Wine: Red Sancerre from the Loire Valley

Chicken Cutlets with Lemon & Capers

SERVINGS: 6

Like many other favorite chicken dishes, this one evolved from an Italian classic traditionally prepared with veal cutlets.

If you can get capers preserved in salt, do, as they make a flavorful difference. I also try to serve caper berries on the side to increase the taste experience. Saffron risotto or buttered steamed rice can be served as an excellent side dish.

2 tablespoons olive oil

3 whole chicken breasts, boned, skinned, halved, and pounded into ¼-inch-thick cutlets

Flour

3 tablespoons dry white wine

3 tablespoons freshly squeezed lemon juice

4 tablespoons unsalted butter

2 tablespoons salted capers preserved in salt, soaked in water for 10 minutes and rinsed a few times (or capers preserved in vinegar, thoroughly rinsed and drained)

Freshly ground pepper

Sea salt

Caper berries (optional)

Heat the oil in a sauté pan.

Dredge the cutlets lightly in the flour, add them to the pan, and cook for 1 to 2 minutes on each side.

Remove the cutlets from the pan and keep them warm in a dish.

Over high heat, add the wine and deglaze the pan. Add the lemon juice and lower the heat; add the butter and stir for 1 minute.

Add the capers and stir for 1 to 2 minutes.

Return the cutlets to the pan and pour in any chicken juices from the dish. Quickly turn the cutlets a few times in the sauce. Season with pepper, taste, and add salt if necessary.

Remove the pan from the heat, place the cutlets on a warm platter, and pour the sauce over. Serve the caper berries on the side.

Suggested Wine: White Chianti

Capers are the buds of a flowering bush that grows throughout Asia and the Mediterranean. They are picked, dried, and pickled, then preserved in brine or salt. Here, a primitive-style chicken-bordered plate bears salted capers from Italy and stemmed caper berries from Spain.

The fabric is called a mola. This handicraft, of the Cuna Indian women of Panama, employs appliqué and decorative stitchwork. To fully appreciate this beautiful work, collectors often use them as wall hangings.

To the Chinese, this rooster talisman carved in jade bears many positive associations. Jade is considered the most precious stone, imbued with the qualities of perfection, purity, and immortality. In Zen teachings the rooster is considered a fit symbol of the five virtues. His comb or crown bestows upon him civic virtue and a literary spirit; his spurs and his fierceness in fighting represent martial virtue and courage; he calls hens to feed and shares with them, thus exhibiting kindness; announcing the dawn with accuracy and regularity, he represents confidence, reliability, and faithfulness. The rooster is also the tenth creature in the Chinese zodiac.

BELOW: This rooster is carved in cinnabar and strung on a tasseled cord. The red rooster is considered good luck and protection against fire. The color red is itself a symbol of joy, used for festive occasions. The endless knot in the cord, positioned above the cock, represents longevity, continuity, and eternity.

Sesame Chicken Fingers

SERVINGS: 4

A variation on a traditional Japanese dish, *goma yaki*, in which toasted sesame seeds are sprinkled on chicken pieces. The dipping sauce is based on Thai cooking. Chinese noodles with peanut sauce, homemade or takeout, would nicely complete this pan-Asian menu.

4 tablespoons sake

1 tablespoon soy sauce

2 whole chicken breasts, boned and skinned, pounded to ¼-inch thickness, cut into 1-inch-wide strips

2 cloves garlic, finely chopped

1 tablespoon plus 1 teaspoon brown sugar

1 small hot red chile pepper (Thai or Serrano), seeded and minced

3 tablespoons fresh lime juice

¼ cup Asian fermented fish sauce

3 tablespoons plus 1 teaspoon rice wine vinegar

2 teaspoons minced lime zest

2 tablespoons finely chopped cilantro

1 tablespoon finely chopped scallion

6 tablespoons sesame seeds

⅔ cup plus 3 tablespoons plain fine dry breadcrumbs

Flour

2 eggs, lightly beaten

1 tablespoon sesame oil

3 tablespoons vegetable oil

Combine the sake and soy sauce in a dish and marinate the chicken slices in the mixture for 30 minutes.

Combine the garlic, brown sugar, and chile in a mortar and pound into a paste; stir in 2 tablespoons of hot water.

In a serving pitcher, combine the paste with the lime juice, fish sauce, and vinegar. Add the lime zest, cilantro, and scallion and let stand for a few hours.

Mix the sesame seeds with the bread crumbs.

Dredge the chicken strips, a few at a time, in the flour, dip them in the eggs, and then coat thoroughly with the bread-crumb mixture.

Heat the oils in a skillet. Fry the strips for 2 minutes on each side or until cooked through and golden brown. As the strips cook, set them aside on a serving dish and keep warm.

Continue until all the chicken has been cooked.

Suggested Wine: Dry white wine from the Loire Valley, such as Sancerre

Chicken Fondue, Bourguignonne Style

—❦—

SERVINGS: 4 TO 6

*F*rom the French and Swiss Alps, where chunks of bread are dipped into pots of bubbling cheese, to Burgundy's fondue of chunks of beef cooked in oil, to the Japanese *shabu-shabu*, in which thin slices of beef and vegetables are cooked in a bubbling broth, fondues are popular meals. Back in the 1970s, these dishes were dinner-party favorites, and at our house always resulted in long, leisurely, sociable meals.

Because of our preference for chicken, an adaptation of the Burgundian version became our fondue of choice. Chunks or strips of chicken breast cooked in a thyme-flavored cooking oil are served with a variety of traditional sauces for dipping, and garnishes of cornichons and pickled onions.

The selection of sauces can be expansive. Mayonnaise, cream, mustard, and tomato—flavored with garlic, herbs, and spices—are the usual bases for bourguignonne sauces, but Asian, Mexican, and Caribbean food also can inspire interesting sauces, salsas, and chutneys to accompany this dish. The good quality of commercial sauces, flavored mustards, and dressings allow even greater flexibility and variety.

Serve a refreshing mixed green salad, dressed in a simple vinaigrette, with or before the fondue.

2 pounds chicken breasts, boned, skinned, and cut into 1-inch or slightly larger chunks, patted dry with paper towels
1½ teaspoons dried thyme
Freshly ground pepper
Vegetable oil to fill the fondue pot
1 or 2 sprigs fresh thyme
Cornichons and pickled onions

Here are some suggestions for easy mayonnaise- and sour cream–based dips. For each, combine the listed ingredients well.

Garlic Mayonnaise

1 cup homemade (see page 159) or store-bought mayonnaise
1 clove elephant garlic or 2 regular cloves garlic, crushed through a garlic press or very finely minced

Smoky Barbecue

1 cup homemade (see page 159) or store-bought mayonnaise
1 tablespoon of your favorite barbecue sauce

Curried Mayonnaise

1 cup homemade (see page 159) or store-bought mayonnaise
2 to 3 teaspoons mild curry powder (or to taste)
1 tablespoon plus 1 teaspoon minced fresh cilantro

Spicy Tomato Mayonnaise

1 cup homemade (see page 159) or
   store-bought mayonnaise

2 tablespoons plain or chili-flavored
   tomato ketchup

Hot red pepper sauce to taste

Mustard Cream

1 cup sour cream

3 to 4 tablespoons Dijon mustard
   (or use a flavored mustard, such as
   nettle, tarragon, horseradish, or
   champagne, and omit the chives)

2 tablespoons minced fresh chives

Season the chicken pieces with the dried
thyme and pepper. Let stand for 20 to
30 minutes, then divide the chicken
equally among individual serving dishes
or bowls.

Pour the oil into the fondue pot and
add the sprig of thyme. Slowly heat the
oil over low to medium heat on the
stovetop for 10 minutes. Test the temperature by dipping one piece of
chicken on a fondue fork into the oil;
the oil is ready if the chicken sizzles.

Bring the pot to its stand and burner
at the table, adjusting the heat to maintain the cooking temperature, without
allowing the oil to burn or smoke.

Serve the chicken, cornichons,
pickled onions, and a selection of
dipping sauces in separate bowls with
spoons. Let each guest cook his or her
own chicken by placing pieces on
a fondue fork and into the oil; the
chicken is usually done by the time
it is lightly browned.

Suggested Wine: Pinot Noir

OPPOSITE: *Santa Fe artist Bob Johnson
designed this cocky rooster in wildly
unnatural color to help brighten a garden.*

BELOW: *"Biscuits St. Michel" have
long been a beloved product of France.
The old Biscuits St. Michel tins are
decorated with a bold graphic that
incorporates wheat motifs and a plump
farm hen in the design—wonderful
finds for the chicken collector.*

4

Stew, Braise & Poach

FOR MOST PEOPLE MANY OF THE DISHES PRODUCED by these methods are emotionally as well as physically satisfying and pleasing. The stews, ragouts, or soups created are hearty and warming and heart-warming memories can float on the cooking aromas that fill the kitchen's air for hours as they gently simmer. I think of such dishes as the supreme mothers of comfort food.

The methods of stewing, braising, and poaching cook food slowly and gently in liquid for relatively long periods of time. In braising, the ingredients are always first browned in a little fat over moderate high heat before the addition of liquid. Less liquid is used and the dish usually simmered longer than when stewing. In braising, large and even whole pieces of meat are cooked, while stewing uses small pieces. In either case the pot is covered in order to utilize not only the heat of the oven or stove top but built-up steam as well. Fricassees are stews with a white sauce. Pot roasting is a combination of braising and stewing—the meat is seared to seal in the juices and is cooked in a fair amount of liquid.

Poaching cooks food in liquid maintained at less than a simmer. Steaming cooks over a boiling liquid in the steam the liquid creates—a steamer basket, or tray keeps the food above the liquid and the pot is covered to keep in the steam. Poaching and steaming are not as commonly used for poultry as those methods.

These methods of cooking with liquid and steam most often produce one-pot dishes of meat and vegetables with their own broth or sauce; poaching or steaming often lead to dishes that have vegetable accompaniments prepared separately.

As all these methods of cooking require a container in which the food can be cooked, they emerge later in culinary history than others. But just when is subject to even more conjecture, supposition, and dispute than the first appearances of roasting or grilling.

The ancestry of today's pots and pans goes back thousands of years and developed from pottery to bronze and then to iron. So it is suggested that the first stews and ragouts probably were cooked in containers provided by nature. Stone-lined

The chickens who call this coop home will surely come home to roost, drawn to the fanciful design of their not-so-humble abode.

Elaborate filigree and scrollwork embellish the front of the coop and a pair of hens flank the entrance in traditional heraldic posture.

pits, large mollusks or reptile shells, or an animal's stomach are proposed to have been the earliest heat- and waterproof equivalents of the pot.

Certainly it is the iron pot that achieved wide-spread use and celebrity. The kettle or cauldron bubbling over an open fire in a primitive dwelling or medieval hall has many historic as well as literary references. It has been greatly valued for centuries as an indispensable item of the kitchen and home. The kettle or cauldron dominated the kitchens of northern countries and everyday cooking until the eighteenth century. It was the most expensive and considered the most important article carried in the covered wagons of the pioneers who settled the American West in the nineteenth century. The iron pot changed little until the developments in materials and design of the twentieth century produced numerous variations on the theme.

All the different methods described, from stewing to steaming, are used for the recipes in this chapter. Most create satisfying one-pot meals, others only the main ingredient for a salad or a sandwich. Some are master recipes with variations that follow the basic procedure and alter the vegetable ingredients or the finished sauce. Simple, home-style dishes as well a few elegant ones meant for special meals are included.

Mom's Chicken in the Pot

Poule au Pot

Pot-au-Feu

Colombian "Pot-au-Feu"

Chicken in Beer

Coq au Vin & Coq au Vin Jaune

Champagne Poussins

Coconut Curry with
Potatoes & Okra

Chicken in Cream Sauce

Chicken Normandy Style

Chicken Couscous

Steaming or Poaching
Chicken Breasts: The Basics

Chicken with Savoy Cabbage

Poached Chicken with Vegetables
& Garlic Mayonnaise Sauce

Pollo Tonnato

Chicken Salads

Mom's Chicken in the Pot

❧

SERVINGS: 4 TO 6

Everyone's mother has a chicken in the pot or soup recipe—it is a dish that nurtures the spirit as well as the body. My mother made this version at least once a week in cool weather. It was such a favorite of mine that I asked her to serve it at my eighteenth birthday party.

The recipe is similar to the recipe for Poule au Pot on page 104, with the following alterations:

For the chicken and broth, increase the quantity of chicken stock from 5 or 6 cups to 7 to 8 cups and omit the peppercorns, adding 3 minced garlic cloves and freshly ground pepper instead. Follow the cooking instructions up to the point the chicken is cooked through, then strip all the chicken meat from the carcass, tear it into small pieces, place the meat in a bowl, and keep it warm.

Serve with the vegetable accompaniment below and egg noodles rather than stuffing.

For the vegetables

- 1 pound carrots, scraped and sliced into ½-inch rounds
- 4 leeks, white and pale green parts only, sliced into rounds and carefully washed
- 2 to 3 medium onions, quartered
- 1 quart chicken broth or stock
- ¾ to 1 pound good-quality broad flat egg noodles
- Olive oil

Cook the vegetables according to the instructions on page 105. Remove the vegetables from the pot and place them in a bowl in the oven to keep warm.

Bring the broth to a rapid boil. Add the egg noodles, and cook according to the directions on the package. Drain the noodles and toss with some olive oil to keep them from sticking together.

Divide the noodles among large soup or stew dishes. Add some of the chicken and vegetables to each dish and top with the piping-hot home-made broth.

Suggested Wine: California Merlot

The tradition of wooden or stone carved animal totems and fetishes centered on the mythical and mystical roots and powers of animals has a long history in Native American folk art.

ABOVE: This rather eccentric little green terra cotta hen is the work of a contemporary folk artist.

OPPOSITE: This charming little hen on her straw nest, by Native American artist Edith John, moves the tradition into an exuberant style that now includes familiar domesticated animals as purely decorative objects made for the contemporary collector.

Poule au Pot

—❧—

SERVINGS: 4 TO 6

This recipe is as traditional a French classic as Sunday lunch itself.

It also has celebrated political connotations and connections. Americans may remember President Herbert Hoover's promise of "a chicken in every pot." The French, as usual, can claim their culinary superiority by some three hundred years, when they quote King Henri IV (who reigned 1589 to 1610): "I want there to be no peasant in my kingdom so poor that he cannot have a chicken in his pot every Sunday." Hoover's chicken was political allegory while Henri's was, and still is, a real dish. My recipe combines the traditional ingredients of poule au pot—chicken, vegetables, soup, and stuffing—with a family recipe.

In my kitchen, when I'm cooking chicken in a broth that becomes part of the dish, no matter what the accompaniments or garnishes, I always start with my mother's method. Whether it was a pot-au-feu, poule au pot, or just chicken in broth with noodles, Mom always said, "You need a good chicken, but the chicken needs good soup greens and bones."

For the chicken and broth

- 4- to 4½-pound whole free-range chicken
- 2 carrots, scraped and cut into 2-inch pieces
- 2 leeks, white and pale green parts only, cut into 2-inch pieces and carefully washed
- 1 small onion, cut into quarters
- ½ cup chopped celery
- 1 small turnip, cut in half
- 2 parsnips, peeled and cut into 2-inch pieces
- Bouquet garni (4 sprigs flat-leaf parsley, 2 or 3 sprigs thyme, and 1 bay leaf tied together)
- 10 to 12 whole black peppercorns
- ¾ pound veal marrowbones (optional; see Note)
- 5 to 6 cups chicken broth or stock

For the stuffing

- 8 ounces chicken sausage meat (see Note)
- 4 ounces prosciutto in one piece, coarsely chopped
- 3 tablespoons chopped fresh flat-leaf parsley
- 2 shallots, chopped
- 2 cloves garlic, minced
- ½ cup fine dry breadcrumbs
- 2 large eggs

For the vegetables

- 1 quart chicken broth or stock
- ¾ pound carrots, peeled and cut in half
- ½ pound turnips, scrubbed and cut into quarters; or ½ pound parsnips, scrubbed and cut into chunks
- 4 to 6 leeks, white and pale green parts only, carefully washed
- 1 small knob celeriac, cut into quarters

For the garnish

- 2 tablespoons unsalted butter
- 4 to 6 (½-inch-thick) slices sourdough bread, crusts removed
- 2 ounces grated Gruyère cheese
- 1½ tablespoons finely chopped fresh flat-leaf parsley

Begin the chicken and broth. Combine the chicken, vegetables, bouquet garni, peppercorns, marrowbones, and prepared broth in a large pot. The liquid should just cover the contents.

Bring to a boil over high heat. Lower the heat, cover, and gently simmer for 50 minutes or until the chicken is cooked through (see page 162). Remove the chicken and set it aside on a warmed platter.

Preheat the oven to 250 degrees or to a "warm" setting.

Strain the broth through a colander or large sieve. Discard the vegetables, return the broth to the pot, and keep at a low simmer.

Carve the chicken into serving pieces, arrange them on the platter, and place it in the oven to keep warm.

While the chicken is cooking, combine all the ingredients for the stuffing in a large bowl and mix thoroughly.

Work the mixture into a log or large sausage shape, and place it on a lightly oiled sheet of heavy-duty aluminum foil. Roll up the foil and secure tightly. Place the stuffing roll into a shallow saucepan and pour in enough water to just cover. Bring to a rapid boil, then immediately lower the heat to maintain a slow boil and cook for 45 minutes or until the sausage meat is cooked through.

Remove the stuffing roll from the pan and set it in the warm oven. When ready to serve, unwrap the stuffing and slice it. Arrange the slices around the carved chicken pieces. Spoon over some broth to moisten.

While the chicken and stuffing are cooking, pour the prepared broth for the vegetables into a large saucepan. Bring to a boil.

Add the vegetables to the pot, lower the heat, and cook for about 20 minutes. Test the vegetables as they simmer, removing those that are cooked as you go. Reserve them on a plate or in a bowl in the warm oven; when ready to serve, arrange them on the platter with the chicken and stuffing.

While the chicken and vegetables are cooking, heat the butter for the garnish in a large skillet. Brown the slices of bread in the butter, remove to a baking sheet, and sprinkle with the cheese.

While the chicken is being carved, preheat the broiler. Place the bread under the broiler and cook until the cheese melts; remove the bread and sprinkle with the parsley.

At our house, we serve the chicken, stuffing, and vegetables in deep plates and moisten everything with a ladleful of hot broth. We also offer portions of piping-hot broth in separate soup bowls and pass the bread at the table.

Alternatively, you can serve the broth as a first course with the bread

This wonderfully colorful hand-painted plate with lush floral border features a rooster and hen in a landscape. It is said to be in the Continental style of the nineteenth century.

floated in each bowl. Follow this with the chicken, stuffing, and vegetables moistened with some broth as a main course.

Suggested Wine: Red Malbec

Notes: Beef marrowbone can be substituted for the veal; either is optional, but their inclusion makes a huge difference in the finished dish. The marrowbones enhance the flavor and richness of the broth, whether you are starting with a homemade or a good-quality purchased broth or stock. For those who enjoy eating the soft marrow, you can also serve the marrowbones as part of the dish.

For the stuffing, you can open chicken sausages from the butcher shop or substitute loose pork sausage meat.

Pot-au-Feu

SERVINGS: 6

Pot-au-feu is another all-in-one-pot dish featuring meat, poultry, and vegetables served in, or accompanied by, the cooking broth. Although the name is French, and it is truly one of France's classic dishes, there are different versions from other places and peoples around the world, usually distinguished by the vegetables and accompanying condiments or relishes.

From the soup to the coarse salt and cornichons, this recipe is based on the basic French-style pot-au-feu.

For the meat and broth

2 tablespoons corn oil

6 chicken thighs

1½ pounds veal marrowbones (see Note, page 105), cut into pieces

1 small turnip, cut in half

2 carrots, scraped and cut into 2-inch pieces

½ cup chopped celery

2 leeks, white and pale green parts only, cut into 2-inch pieces and carefully washed

1 small onion, cut into quarters

3 cloves garlic, minced

Bouquet garni (4 sprigs flat-leaf parsley, 2 or 3 sprigs thyme, and 1 bay leaf tied together)

2 to 2½ pounds beef shank in one piece

3 quarts chicken broth or stock

Freshly ground pepper

For the vegetables

1 head savoy cabbage, cut into 6 wedges and cored

6 leeks, trimmed, including some green parts, carefully washed

8 to 10 carrots, scraped and cut into 2-inch pieces

4 cups chicken broth or stock

Coarse sea salt or kosher salt

Cornichons

Begin the meat and broth. Heat the oil in a 7-quart (or larger) saucepan, add the chicken thighs, and cook until golden brown on all sides; remove the thighs from the pan and set aside.

Add the marrowbones, turnip, carrots, celery, leeks, onion, garlic, bouquet garni, and beef. Pour in the broth to cover. Season with pepper.

Bring to a boil over high heat, lower the heat to a simmer, cover, and cook for 1 hour.

While the beef is cooking, steam the cabbage in a microwave oven or in a steamer for 6 to 8 minutes or until it is barely tender; set aside.

Add the chicken to the beef and continue to simmer for an additional 30 to 35 minutes.

While the chicken and beef are cooking, pour the prepared broth for the vegetables into a separate saucepan and bring to a boil. Add the leeks and simmer for 10 to 15 minutes. Add the carrots and cook for 8 minutes more. Add the cabbage and 2 ladlesfull of the broth from the pot with the meats and cook for 5 minutes more. Remove the pot from the heat and cover.

When the chicken and beef are ready, remove them and the marrowbones from the pot.

Strain the broth through a colander, and return the liquid to the pot over medium heat to keep it hot.

Carve the beef into serving pieces.

Using a slotted spoon, divide the vegetables among large soup or stew bowls. Serve the beef, marrowbones, and chicken thighs on top.

Ladle a good portion of broth into the bowls and serve. Pass the salt and cornichons at the table and offer more soup as the meal progresses.

Suggested Wine: Red Burgundy, such as Châteauneuf du Pape

The tureen, a deep covered dish used for the serving of soups and stews, can be traced back to primitively designed ancient communal bowls and medieval cauldrons. The word itself may be a corruption of terrin, from the Old French, which referred specifically to a pottery vessel.

However, it was not until the eighteenth century that the tureen blossomed into the beautiful and decorative pieces we're familiar with today. Fashioned in ceramics or even from precious metal, the soup tureen became appreciated as an object of great luxury.

Tureen designs depicting vegetable and animal forms, particularly birds and fowl, were common throughout Europe at this time. They originated in Germany with the porcelains of Meissen and the faience of Hochst, designs that came of age during the elaborate and elegant Rococo period.

The Chelsea Porcelain Manufactory is reputed to have produced the finest wares in all of England. The Hen and Chicks tureen shown here, made of soft-paste porcelain around 1755, is from Chelsea's red-anchor period, the high point of the company's technical and design achievements.

Photo courtesy of Winterthur Museum; from the Campbell Collection of soup tureens at Winterthur.

Colombian "Pot-au-Feu"

SERVINGS: 6

This is purported to be a Colombian version of pot-au-feu, passed on to me in the true oral tradition. A dear friend of my mother (of Italian origins, who lived in Egypt and spent time in South America) served this to my parents for dinner one evening at her home in Florida. The recipe was recited to my mother when she inquired after it, and she passed her memory of it by telephone to me.

Use the recipe for the French-style pot-au-feu on page 106, making only this change to the meat and broth: Substitute 4 sprigs of fresh cilantro for the parsley in the bouquet garni. The vegetable accompaniment gives this recipe its Colombian character.

For the vegetables

- 4 cups vegetable or chicken broth or stock
- 12 to 16 cipollini onions or small boiling onions, peeled
- 3 ears fresh sweet corn, cut into 2-inch rounds
- 2 to 3 yams or sweet potatoes, peeled and cut into large chunks
- 2 ripe avocados, peeled, pitted, and sliced
- 1 cup sour cream

Bring the broth to a boil, add the onions, and cook for about 20 minutes. Add the corn and cook for 8 to 10 minutes until tender.

Place the yams in a separate pot of water and bring to a boil. Lower the heat and cook for 10 to 15 minutes or until tender. Drain the yams and add them to the onions and corn to keep warm.

Using a slotted spoon, divide the vegetables among 6 large soup or stew bowls. Serve the beef, marrow-bones, and chicken thighs on top. Ladle a good portion of broth into the bowls, garnish with fresh cilantro, and serve. Pass avocado slices and sour cream at the table and offer more soup as the meal progresses.

Suggested Wine: Cabernet Sauvignon from Chile

CLOCKWISE FROM CENTER: *The tall stemmed wine glass bearing a brightly colored rooster was hand-painted by a contemporary artist. Next to it a gold-rimmed wine glass from a much earlier date contrasts in design, but not technique. The mass-produced juice glass with a one-color silhouetted design is graphic simplicity—decidedly collectible kitsch. In contrast, the hand-painted tumbler renders the rooster in greater detail. A cranberry glass goblet also shows quality of detail in its clear chicken-shaped pedestal.*

Chicken in Beer

*T*here is a long-standing tradition of stewed beef and pork recipes that call for all sorts of beer—from lagers to stouts. Often dried fruit, such as prunes, raisins, apricots, or a mixture, is added, along with a garnish of chopped nuts. This recipe adapts one of my favorite beef stews to chicken. It's great served on a bed of thick egg noodles or with multi-grain bread slices topped with a hearty veined cheese, like Shropshire Blue, melted under the broiler.

The old fashioned drinking jar is reproduced in blue-tinted glass impressed with a rooster motif. It retains its screw top for a lid but features a mug-style handle for ease. A "jar" is also a measure and is a colloquial term for a glass of beer. Originally, they were simply ordinary jars used for drinking.

2 tablespoons corn oil

2 bay leaves

4 large chicken legs, drumstick
    ends chopped off

1 large sweet onion (about 1¼ pounds),
    peeled and thickly sliced

2 tablespoons flour

½ pint stout

1½ cups chicken broth or stock

¼ teaspoon sea salt

Freshly ground pepper

⅛ teaspoon dried thyme

10 ounces baby carrots

6 ounces prunes, pitted and cut in half

1 to 2 tablespoons unsalted butter
    (optional)

1 to 2 tablespoons flour (optional)

2 tablespoons chopped flat-leaf parsley

Heat the oil in a flameproof casserole or Dutch oven. Add the bay leaves and gently sauté, turning over, for 1 to 2 minutes.

Add the chicken legs a piece or two at a time and brown on all sides. Remove the chicken pieces and set them aside.

Add the onion slices to the casserole and cook them on both sides until they are a light golden color.

Sprinkle the onions with the flour and brown.

Return the chicken pieces to the casserole with the onions. Pour in the stout and just enough broth to cover; add more broth if needed. Season with the salt, pepper, and the thyme.

Bring the liquid to a boil over high heat, then lower the heat, cover, and gently simmer for 20 minutes.

Add the carrots and continue cooking for an additional 10 minutes. Add the prunes and cook for 15 to 20 minutes longer or until the chicken is cooked through (see page 162) and the carrots are tender. Discard the bay leaves.

If you like your stew sauces thick and creamy, proceed as follows: When the chicken and carrots are done, ladle some of the liquid from the casserole into a measuring cup. For each cup of liquid, work 1 tablespoon each of flour and butter together with your fingers or a fork into a smooth paste (a *beurre manié*). Whisk the *beurre manié* into the liquid in the measuring cup, then pour it back into the casserole and gently stir it into the other ingredients.

Sprinkle with the parsley and serve piping hot.

Suggested Beverage: Rich stout, such as Guinness or Murphy's, or a hearty red wine, such as Cabernet Sauvignon from Oregon State

Coq au Vin & Coq au Vin Jaune

—🐓—

SERVINGS: 6

This is a dish with a centuries-long history, and perhaps nearly as many variations as there are professional chefs or home cooks who have prepared it. Some marinate, others do not. The method of cooking varies—on the stovetop or in the oven. Some cooks include lardons (an addition attributed to none other than Julius Caesar), onions, or mushrooms; sometimes these are cooked with the chicken, sometimes braised separately and added at the end. Some recipes suggest that the flambé of an alcohol is an optional step. And thickening and smoothing out the sauce at the end can be achieved by incorporating chicken's blood, a *beurre manié* (see page 109), or cocoa powder—a highly original method.

And then, to be sure, there is the question of what kind of wine to use. Tradition says this dish was first created in the Auvergne region of south central France, using a local wine called Chanturgues, defined in *Schoonmaker's Encyclopedia of Wine* as a "small, pleasant Gamay, a hard-to-find *vin de pays*." In fact, the choice of local or regional wines for coq au vin is very prevalent. Most people think that a Burgundy must be used in this dish—as did I until recently. Therefore, the first of these two coq au vin recipes is made with just that. (It is equally good with a California Cabernet Sauvignon, which I have used on occasion.) But the second version, my favorite coq au vin, uses a very special and unusual wine, Vin Jaune. From the Jura in France, this wine has a character not unlike a very light sherry. The slow process used in its production gives it a distinctive quality and, unfortunately, a high price tag, but the results when used in this dish are well worth it—at least for a special-occasion dinner.

You must begin to marinate the chicken the day before cooking.

1 large onion, chopped

2 large shallots, chopped

2 large cloves garlic, crushed with the flat of a knife

3 carrots, scraped and chopped

Bouquet garni (4 sprigs of flat-leaf parsley, 2 or 3 sprigs thyme, and 1 bay leaf tied together)

1 (750-ml) bottle red wine (Burgundy or California Cabernet Sauvignon)

6-pound free-range chicken, cut into 10 pieces

Sea salt

Freshly ground pepper

3 to 4 tablespoons vegetable oil

4 tablespoons flour

⅓ cup cognac

3 to 6 tablespoons unsalted butter

½ pound smoked bacon, cut into lardons (see page 90)

24 pearl onions, peeled

1 pound small cremini mushroom caps (about the size of a quarter), halved, or quartered if larger

In a large bowl or nonreactive baking dish, combine the onion, shallots, garlic, carrots, and the bouquet garni. Add the wine and stir. Add the chicken pieces and turn to coat thoroughly. Cover and refrigerate overnight.

Remove the chicken pieces from the marinade, reserving the marinade.

Wipe away any bits of marinade vegetables from the chicken and pat it dry, then season with salt and pepper.

Heat the oil in a flameproof casserole or Dutch oven. Add the chicken a few pieces at a time and cook until evenly golden on all sides; remove the pieces to a platter and set aside.

Add 2 tablespoons of the flour to the casserole and cook for 2 to 3 minutes, stirring constantly; remove from the heat.

Heat the cognac in a separate saucepan or in a microwave oven.

Return the chicken pieces to the casserole, add the cognac and light it with a match. When the flames have subsided, put the casserole back on the heat and add the reserved marinade.

Bring the liquid to a boil over high heat. Lower the heat to maintain a simmer and cook, partially covered, for 1½ hours or until the chicken is done (see page 162).

While the chicken is simmering, preheat the oven to 350 degrees.

In a sauté pan heat 1 tablespoon of the butter and cook the lardons until golden and crisp. Remove the lardons from the pan with a slotted spoon and set aside.

Add the pearl onions to the pan and cook, shaking the pan constantly, until they are slightly browned on all sides. Remove the onions from the pan with a slotted spoon and put them in a baking dish in one layer; bake in the oven for 20 minutes.

Meanwhile, add more butter to the pan if necessary, and sauté the mushrooms until tender; set aside.

When the chicken is done, remove the pieces from the casserole and set them aside on a warmed dish.

Pour the chicken cooking liquid through a sieve into a large measuring cup and discard all the solid bits. Pour the liquid back into the casserole and bring to a boil.

In a small mixing bowl, work 2 tablespoons of the flour into 2 tablespoons of the butter to form a smooth paste.

Remove the casserole from the heat. Whisk some of the hot sauce into the bowl with the flour and butter mixture. When the mixture is smooth, whisk it into the sauce in the casserole and blend until smooth and thoroughly incorporated.

Drain the onions, mushrooms, and lardons. Return the casserole to the heat, add the chicken, vegetables, and lardons. Bring to a simmer to heat through; serve.

Suggested Wine: For Coq au Vin, Nuit St. George; for Coq au Vin Jaune, Richebourg

Variation

Coq au Vin Jaune

Follow the recipe for Coq au Vin, substituting 6 plump legs with their bone ends trimmed, which makes for a very elegant presentation. (Chicken breasts on the bone also can be used.) For the wine, use one bottle Vin Jaune and ⅓ cup unflavored eau de vie or vodka.

Blue and white ceramics were also popular and prolifically produced in France and England with European as well as Asian influenced designs. This contemporary plate's pattern is reproduced in the antique way, stamped with copper plates on which the design was hand engraved.

Champagne Poussins

SERVINGS: 4

*T*his is a recipe from my husband's uncle Yves Auzolle, a gifted chef. A very simple but elegant dish, it was one for which he and his Parisian restaurant, La Truite (circa 1950s), were celebrated. Yves's preferred accompaniment for this dish was sautéed potatoes and separately sautéed mushrooms.

For the chicken in Yves's original *coquelet au champagne*, I use poussins.

½ cup unsalted butter

½ pound salt pork, cut into lardons (see page 90)

½ pound small (about 1-inch in diameter) white onions, peeled, bottoms scored

2 whole poussins

Sea salt

Freshly ground pepper

⅓ cup cognac

1 (750-ml) bottle dry champagne

Melt the butter in an enameled cast-iron casserole or Dutch oven. Add the lardons and onions and cook until lightly golden on all sides.

Add the poussins and brown on all sides. Season with salt and pepper.

Heat the cognac in a small saucepan or in a microwave oven. Sprinkle the cognac over the contents of the casserole and light it with a match. When the flames have subsided, pour in the champagne and cook over medium heat for 30 minutes or until the chicken is done (see page 162). Using a slotted spoon, remove the poussins, onions, and lardons to a platter and keep warm. Reduce the liquid in the casserole by half.

Cut the poussins in half, arrange on a serving platter surrounded by the onions and lardons, and pour the sauce over.

Suggested Wine: Pomerol

---

*T*he elegant dish of Champagne Poussins makes dinner a special occasion and perhaps a romantic evening for two. The brass statuettes of proud stanced chickens from the late nineteenth and early twentieth centuries, and the prominent faux stone rooster, reflect in the glow of candlelight and echo the metallic colors in the damask tablecloth.

Coconut Curry with Potatoes and Okra

SERVINGS: 6 TO 8

My first exposure to Indian cuisine occurred when I lived in England in the mid-1970s. In those days, if you loved good food, dining out meant fine cuisine at top prices or, for informal and affordable dining, the best bets were some—but not all—of the pubs and neighborhood Indian eateries, which offered authentic as well as anglicized dishes. Anglicized curry is, perhaps, an early example of "fusion" cuisine. I have eaten countless curries over the years and, as the saying goes, I haven't met one I didn't like. This one has a softly aromatic and slightly sweet character.

To increase the heat, substitute additional hot curry powder for the mild.

6 chicken breasts, boned, skinned,
    and halved (12 pieces) cut into
    ¾-inch pieces
1 tablespoon vegetable oil
1 onion, chopped
1 clove elephant garlic, finely chopped
    (about 2 tablespoons)
3 tablespoons mild curry powder
1 tablespoon hot curry powder
1 teaspoon ground ginger
½ teaspoon ground coriander
¾ teaspoon sea salt
2 tablespoons flour
1½ cups chicken broth or stock
1½ cups unsweetened canned coconut milk
1 tablespoon desiccated coconut
    (or organic coconut flakes, which
    are much less sweet)

2 white potatoes (about 1 pound),
    peeled and cut into ½-inch dice
½ cup chopped fresh cilantro
10 ounces fresh or frozen okra

In a nonstick sauté pan, sauté the chicken pieces until they no longer have a raw look and take on a white color all over, but do not brown. Remove the chicken.

Heat the oil in a flameproof casserole or Dutch oven. Add the onion and cook until translucent, about 4 minutes.

Add the garlic, curry powders, ginger, coriander, and ½ teaspoon of the salt. Stir for 1 minute.

Sprinkle the flour over the spice mixture and quickly stir to combine.

Pour in the broth and coconut milk and stir. Add the dried coconut; mix well and bring to a simmer.

Add the potatoes and cook over low heat for 10 to 12 minutes or until almost tender.

Add the chicken, cover, and simmer for 8 minutes. Stir in the cilantro and cook for 2 minutes.

Meanwhile, cook fresh okra in a saucepan of boiling water for 8 to 10 minutes, or cook frozen okra in a microwave oven for 5 minutes on high. Add the okra to the casserole and combine thoroughly.

Simmer the curry for an additional 3 to 5 minutes. Turn off the heat and let stand for 2 minutes before serving.

Suggested Wine: Chilled white, such as Rully

*I*n Hindu legend the cock is referred to as the "rooster king," his morning song a call to roosters all over the world to join in.

A tureen makes an ideal and presentable serving piece for any sort of stew. This one is part of a matched table service, hand-painted with a cocky chicken and stylized floral design from Italy.

Chicken in Cream Sauce

SERVINGS: 8

Traditional dishes can have numerous "authentic" versions. One example is *poulet blanquette*, a basic French recipe of chicken simmered in wine and stock, and finished with a creamy white sauce. The oldest recipes feature an egg and cream mixture to finish the sauce, while the newer ones often do not. Sometimes small white onions or button mushrooms, or both, are included. My version is based on two of my French family's recipes—one for chicken and the other for veal in cream sauce. This combination, with onions and mushrooms, and chunks of boneless, skinless chicken breast, more closely resembles a classic *blanquette de veau à l'ancienne* in its consistency and texture. To enjoy all of the delicate sauce, serve the *blanquette* on a bed of fluffy steamed white rice or broad egg noodles.

It is important that the chicken pieces, mushroom caps, and onions all be about the same size. Bite-sized pieces are perfect for optimum taste, texture, and balance in this dish.

For the onions and mushrooms

- 2 tablespoons unsalted butter, softened
- 2 sprigs fresh flat-leaf parsley
- 1 sprig fresh thyme
- 1 cup chicken broth or stock
- 1 cup dry white wine
- 18 to 24 small (about 1 inch in diameter) white onions, peeled, bottoms scored with a knife
- ¾ pound small cremini mushroom caps (or if large, halved or quartered)

For the chicken and sauce

- 3 pounds boneless, skinless chicken breasts, cut into 1- to 1½-inch cubes
- Vegetable oil
- Freshly ground white pepper
- ¼ teaspoon dried thyme
- 4 tablespoons unsalted butter, softened
- 5 tablespoons flour
- 3 cups chicken stock
- ½ cup dry white wine
- ½ teaspoon sea salt
- 3 egg yolks
- ½ cup heavy cream

Combine the butter, parsley and thyme sprigs, chicken broth, and wine in a sauté pan; stir. Add the onions in one layer. Cover, bring to a simmer, and cook for 25 minutes. Remove the onions with a slotted spoon and set them aside in another bowl.

Add the mushroom caps to the pan and simmer for about 8 minutes. Remove the mushrooms with a slotted spoon and set aside in a bowl.

Pour the cooking liquid through a sieve into a measuring cup and reserve.

In a lightly oiled nonstick sauté pan or skillet, cook the chicken pieces over medium heat, just until all sides of the chicken no longer look raw and are white overall, but not golden or browned, about 5 minutes. Immediately remove the chicken from the pan, transferring the pieces to a bowl. Season with white pepper and the dried thyme.

Melt the butter in an enameled cast-iron casserole or Dutch oven. Add the flour and stir to combine over low heat, 2 to 3 minutes, or until the flour is cooked; do not let the mixture brown.

Remove the casserole from the heat and whisk in the broth, wine, and ⅓ cup of the reserved liquid.

Return the casserole to the heat and bring to a boil. Lower the heat and simmer for 10 minutes, stirring occasionally.

Add the mushrooms, and cook for 6 minutes. Add the chicken, and cook for 10 minutes. Stir in the onions and cook 5 to 8 minutes, or until the chicken is done (see page 162).

Meanwhile, blend the egg yolks and cream in a bowl; whisk the mixture until it is smooth and creamy.

Stir some of the sauce from the casserole into the egg mixture, a few tablespoons at a time; blend well.

Remove the casserole from the heat and slowly pour in the egg and cream mixture, stirring constantly to mix the sauces together thoroughly.

Serve the chicken, onions, and mushrooms on a bed of rice or egg noodles and top with the sauce.

Suggested Wine: Petit Chablis

Antique culinary molds in a variety of figurative forms are highly sought after; those from the 1920s and 1930s are not difficult to find. Made of iron, tin, copper, or wood, they often depict wild or domesticated animals. The chicken is well represented.

Here, a large double-sided mold for shaping three-dimensional chocolate roosters was made in late-nineteenth-century France for export to the British market. The small mold was made in the 1920s for ice cream.

The new napkin ring is a hen fashioned in metal. The design on the placemats and napkins is in the style of antique engravings.

The custom of commissioning portraits of prized livestock and cherished pets grew as animals came to be regarded as valued property, and by extension an expression of a farmer's worth. By the nineteenth century in America, this work was produced primarily by artists whose identities were not recorded, but important painters such as Edward Hicks accepted such commissions.

The chicken of course was among the prime subjects. Barnyard fowl appeared in family portraits, landscapes, and specific poultry vignettes. Prize-winning birds and celebrated breeds of birds were commemorated in individual portraits.

Journals and texts devoted to the art and improvement of animal husbandry were filled with beautiful and artistic illustrations of prized and prize-winning livestock. In England, Cassell's Book of Poultry recorded the winners of farm fairs and animal competitions. Today, Cassell is a source for collectors of antique colored lithographic poultry prints. One artist, Robert Ludlow, was considered such a master of the genre that he was said to have been commissioned for a portrait of an American turkey that was specially shipped to England for his sittings.

LEFT: A signed Ludlow illustration of the fanciful Silver Spangled Polish breed.

FOLLOWING PAGES: On a fireplace mantle, an elegant display of colored engravings from illustrated nineteenth-century journals devoted to farming and livestock, particularly poultry. Today, such prints are highly collectible and, often, quite valuable.

Chicken Normandy Style

SERVINGS: 6

Here is a traditional dish from the Normandy region of France that capitalizes on two of its most famous products: calvados, a fine apple brandy, and apple cider.

This dish has always been an autumn favorite at our house, but is even more so now that we live in upstate New York, where a great variety of wonderful-tasting apples are plentiful. We often make an outing to pick our own apples and serve this dish in the evening followed by a fresh apple crumble. The recipe is based on a family classic, with only the variety of apples changed to capitalize on our local produce.

7 tablespoons unsalted butter
Olive oil
6 chicken legs
Sea salt
Freshly ground pepper
¼ cup calvados or other apple brandy
½ cup cider vinegar
½ cup hard cider or fresh apple cider
1 pound Macoun apples or other tart variety, peeled, cored, and sliced into eighths, tossed with the juice of 1 lemon to prevent discoloring
1 tablespoon powdered sugar
1 tablespoon crème fraîche or sour cream

Preheat the oven to a low warming temperature.

Heat 2 tablespoons of the butter in a pan, add the chicken pieces, and sauté until golden brown on all sides; add some oil if needed to finish browning all the pieces. Remove the chicken from the pan and set aside on a platter. Season with salt and pepper.

Place the pan over low heat and scrape it with a spatula to loosen any browned bits. Sprinkle the pan with the calvados, let it warm, then light it with a match.

When the flames have subsided, add the vinegar and bring to a boil over medium heat; boil for about 5 minutes.

Pour in the cider, bring to a boil, then return the chicken pieces to the pan and cook over medium heat for 30 to 35 minutes or until done (see page 162). Remove the chicken from the pan to a sewing platter in a warm spot. Set the pan with the cooking liquid aside.

About halfway through the cooking time, heat 3 tablespoons of the butter in a skillet, add the apples, season with salt, pepper, and the powdered sugar, and cook until tender, 3 to 5 minutes.

Add the apples to the serving platter; place the platter in the warmed oven.

Place the pan with the chicken cooking liquid over low heat, add any juices from the apple skillet, and slowly reduce the liquid.

Cut the remaining 2 tablespoons of the butter into small pieces and stir it into the sauce; add the crème fraîche and whisk together thoroughly.

Spoon the sauce over the chicken and apples and serve.

Suggested Beverage: French cider or white Loire, such as Gros Plant

My husband gave me this diamanté pin in a rooster design by Dorothy Bauer to celebrate this book—the perfect gift. An endearing detail is the loose, jeweled tail feathers that move freely and create a sparkling effect.

Chicken Couscous

SERVINGS: 6 TO 8

Couscous is a traditional Middle Eastern dish that features steamed semolina and various vegetables with different combinations of mixed meats. Colonial connections with North Africa have made it a part of French cuisine. Certainly, it is a favorite dish of the Arnaud family. My husband Michel often prepares this couscous for larger gatherings of family or friends. This is his recipe, reduced to a manageable 6 to 8 servings.

Merguez is a spicy Middle Eastern sausage; try to find some, but if necessary Cajun andouille can be substituted. Harissa is a hot pepper paste that is packed into tubes and is available in specialty food shops.

1½-pound eggplant

Sea salt

4 tablespoons olive oil

2 medium (about ¾ pound) onions, finely sliced

4 cloves garlic, chopped

3 pounds chicken pieces, thighs and drumsticks

4 medium carrots, scraped and cut into chunks

1 red bell pepper, seeded and cut into 6 strips

1 green bell pepper, seeded and cut into 6 strips

3¼ cups chicken broth or stock

1 tablespoon harissa, plus additional for the table

1 (1 pound, 12 ounce) can whole peeled tomatoes

2 small fresh tomatoes (½ pound), quartered

2¼ pounds zucchini, peeled in stripes and cut into ½-inch rounds

1 (15-ounce) can chickpeas, rinsed and drained

Freshly ground pepper

1½ pounds medium couscous (see Note)

1 tablespoon unsalted butter

1½ pounds merguez or Cajun andouille

1½ duck breasts, boneless (optional)

Peel and cut the eggplant into 2-inch rounds and then into quarters. Place the eggplant pieces on a large plate in one layer. Generously salt them and let them stand for 20 minutes. Rinse the pieces and pat them dry with paper towels; set aside.

Heat the oil in a large flameproof casserole over medium heat. Add the onions and garlic and cook until the onions are translucent and soft. Add the chicken pieces, browning them evenly on all sides until golden, 8 to 10 minutes. Remove the chicken and set aside.

Add the carrots, eggplant, and peppers and cook for a few minutes.

Meanwhile, pour the broth into a large measuring cup or pitcher and whisk in the harissa.

Add the liquid to the casserole and bring to a boil over high heat. Lower the heat and simmer for 10 minutes. Add the tomatoes and zucchini, and return the chicken to the casserole. Season with salt and pepper.

Cover and cook over medium heat for 15 minutes. Add the chickpeas and cook for 5 to 10 minutes longer or until the chicken is done (see page 162).

Place the couscous in a large bowl. Bring 2 cups of water to a boil and immediately pour it over the couscous.

Stir with a fork; mix in the butter.

Transfer the couscous to a *couscoussière* or steamer. When the chicken is done, uncover the casserole and place the *couscoussière* on top. Let the couscous steam for 10 to 15 minutes.

While the chicken, vegetables, and couscous are cooking, prepare and heat the grill or a grill pan.

Grill the *merguez* and duck breasts until cooked through, 15 to 20 minutes.

Serve the couscous in bowls, topped with the chicken, vegetables, and any liquid remaining. Slice the grilled meats into portions and serve at the table from a heated platter. Offer a small bowl of harissa for those who want to add more heat to the dish.

Note: Couscous is semolina pasta formed into tiny pellets. Packaged couscous should be marked with the size of these pellets, usually fine or medium. If possible, purchase the medium size for this recipe.

Suggested Wine: Moroccan red wine, such as Boulaone, or Côte de Provence

Rich, earthy colors often associated with Southwestern and Mexican pottery are the common denominator for a collection of primitive and folk-styled earthen- and stoneware pieces.

The incised stoneware salt and pepper shakers possess a primitive design. The abstract hen motif in the center of the soup bowl (by Peggy Ganstad) and the prominent sunflower pattern on the chicken-shaped planter share the naïf quality of folk art.

Steaming or Poaching Chicken Breasts: The Basics

—❦—

Use these methods to cook boneless, skinless chicken breasts for the recipes that follow. Use any combination of herbs and minced vegetables as flavoring.

2 whole boneless, skinless chicken breasts

Water or chicken broth or stock

Sprigs of fresh herbs such as thyme, tarragon, and flat-leaf parsley (optional)

1 to 2 tablespoons minced vegetables such as carrot and onion (optional)

Remove the tenderloin from the chicken breasts. Pound the breasts lightly to an even thickness.

To poach: Place a medium-sized saucepan of water or broth over medium heat, add the herbs and vegetables, if using, and bring to a boil. Place the chicken breasts in the liquid, adjust the heat to maintain a very low simmer—the surface of the liquid should be no more than quivering—and cook for 12 to 15 minutes or until done (see page 162).

Alternatively, bring the liquid to a boil, place the chicken breasts in the liquid, cover the pan, and immediately remove from the heat. Let the chicken stand in the water for 18 to 20 minutes or until done (see page 162).

Remove the chicken from the liquid and wipe off any herbs or vegetables. Serve immediately, or let the chicken cool to room temperature, cover, and refrigerate until ready to use.

To steam: Place the herbs and vegetables, if using, in a steamer basket and arrange the chicken breasts on top. Pour water or broth into a saucepan large enough to hold the steamer basket; bring to a boil. Set the steamer basket over the boiling liquid (the level of the liquid should come to just below the bottom of the steamer). Steam the chicken breasts for 20 to 25 minutes or until done (see page 162).

Remove the chicken from the steamer and wipe off any herbs or vegetables. Serve immediately, or let the chicken cool to room temperature, cover, and refrigerate until ready to use.

Note: On average, half a boned and skinned chicken breast will yield ¾ cup diced meat; one whole breast yields 1½ cups.

OPPOSITE: *Pendulum operated toys were known as early as 3000 B.C., often with the motif of pecking birds like chickens, a constant favorite of central Europe. On the tin trunk, left: chickens are pegged to a disk attached to a pendulum; its rotation makes the hens peck for grain. Far right, nineteenth-century French hens and chicks feed from a seed pan. To the back, a mock cock fight is set in motion by springs in the base.*

Pull or push toys date back to ancient Egypt, and animal motifs were popular. They were first carved in wood and painted; later cast-iron wheels were used and, in time, the figures made in tin or iron.

On the mat at left, a wooden pull-along rooster; the toy at right has a wheeled stick that sets the baby chicks in motion. Both are French and pre-WWII. To the front, a battery-operated tin hen lays eggs; earlier versions would have been designed as wind-up toys.

BELOW: *A Victorian wooden rooster painted in a stylized manner rolls along on wheels and is propelled by a long handle.*

Chicken delights in this array of objects of artistry or utility:

A pottery bowl has a cutout and painted image of the hen; chickens crafted from bristles are made to hang as ornaments (as seen resting against pottery bowl and also hanging from drawer pull at center, below); a hen's head is a kitchen timer; a ceramic rooster cabinet handle (a hen version is at the far right); wooden rooster with tin tail hanging ornament; hand-crafted folk art speckled hen has a drawer at the bottom; a ceramic spoon rest designed as a hen; boxes printed with chicken landscapes reproduce an antique painting genre; oil jug with cock motif; ornamental kitchen plaque with rooster design and antique finish. The nesting hen is an antique covered dish specifically designed for jam; rooster-headed knives for spreads peek out from a box next to printed napkins and a napkin holder with chicken motifs; the ever-popular rooster head jugs; an antique crocheted potholder is in the shape of a hen; the framed antique rooster is from a Victorian German paper scrapbook. The hen print is nineteenth-century French.

Chicken with Savoy Cabbage

—🐓—

SERVINGS: 4

1 tablespoon peppercorns

1 tablespoon sweet paprika

4 chicken legs

8 medium-sized cipollini onions, or small boiling onions, peeled and pricked all over with a fork

¼ cup plus 2 tablespoons sherry vinegar

1½ heads savoy cabbage (about 1¾ to 2 pounds), cored and cut into ½-inch slices

1 tablespoon unsalted butter

4 ounces pancetta (or slab bacon), cut into ¼-inch strips

1 tablespoon vegetable oil

1½ cups chicken broth or stock

Crack the peppercorns with a pestle in a mortar or by pressing them under the flat side of the blade of a large chef's knife. Combine the cracked pepper with the paprika in bowl. Rub the mixture over the chicken legs. Place the chicken in a baking dish, cover with plastic wrap, and refrigerate for 2 to 3 hours; bring the chicken back to room temperature before proceeding.

Place the onions in a bowl, add the 2 tablespoons of vinegar, pour in just enough water to cover, and soak the onions for about 1 hour. Put the onions and the liquid in a saucepan over medium heat, bring to a low boil, and cook for 5 to 8 minutes—they should be only par-boiled—then drain and set aside.

Blanch the cabbage in a large pot of boiling water, drain, refresh under cold water, and drain again. Set aside.

Heat the butter in a large skillet. Add the pancetta and cook for 3 to 5 minutes.

Add the onions and cook for 5 minutes more, or until the pancetta is browned and crisp. Remove the pancetta and onions from the pan and set aside.

Add the oil to the skillet if needed and heat. Shake off any excess marinade from the chicken legs, add them to the pan, and brown on all sides. Remove the chicken and set it aside on a platter.

Pour the remaining vinegar into the hot pan and scrape up any browned bits; bring the vinegar to a boil.

Add the broth and return to a boil. Mix in the cabbage so it is thoroughly coated with the liquid in the pan.

Add the chicken, onions, and pancetta to the cabbage, cover, and cook over medium heat for 30 minutes or until the chicken is done (see page 162) and the cabbage is very tender.

Suggested Wine: Burgundy, such as Mercurey

Poached Chicken with Vegetables & Garlic Mayonnaise Sauce

SERVINGS: 4

Aïoli is the garlic mayonnaise sauce typically served with steamed fish and vegetables. Along with bouillabaisse and bourride, the classic seafood stews, it is traditional to the cooking of the south of France along the Mediterranean. Aïoli also refers to a dish of poached ingredients served with the mayonnaise. At our house we enjoy it with fish or chicken and seasonal fresh vegetables prepared to their best advantage. Aïoli can be served hot, warm, or at room temperature.

2 to 3 cloves garlic, crushed through a garlic press or ground to a paste in a mortar with a pestle

1 egg yolk

¼ teaspoon salt

⅔ cup olive oil

⅓ cup peanut or corn oil

½ to 1 tablespoon freshly squeezed lemon juice

1 pound small new potatoes, peeled

1 small head (or ½ large) cauliflower, broken into florets

4 large carrots, peeled and cut in half lengthwise, then in thirds crosswise

16 thin spears asparagus

¾ to 1 pound haricots verts or tender young green beans, trimmed

2 whole chicken breasts, boned, skinned, and halved (4 pieces), poached or steamed, preferably with some basil leaves (see page 125)

In a mixing bowl, blend the garlic, egg yolk, and salt together. Mix the two oils together, then very slowly add the oil to the bowl in a steady stream, stirring constantly with a wooden spoon. As the sauce thickens, add a few drops of lemon juice and continue adding the oil until the mixture reaches the consistency of mayonnaise. Taste for seasoning. Set aside in a cool place.

Put the potatoes in a saucepan of cold, salted water. Bring to a boil and cook for about 20 minutes or until tender but not mushy.

Pour some water into a shallow pan and set a steamer basket in the pan; the water should just reach the bottom of the basket. Place the cauliflower in the steamer, cover, and cook for 3 to 5 minutes or until just tender.

Cook the carrots in just enough boiling water to come halfway up their sides for 6 to 8 minutes or until tender.

Place the asparagus in a pan of water, cover, bring to a low boil, then uncover and simmer for 3 to 4 minutes or until tender.

Cook the haricots verts in boiling water for 3 to 4 minutes or until tender.

Arrange the chicken breasts and the vegetables on a large platter with a bowl of the aïoli and let your guests serve themselves.

Suggested Wine: Dry rosé, such as Côte de Provence

OPPOSITE: *A hooked rug uses bold geometric elements as a border and in alternation with the rooster motifs as a pattern for a runner or wall hanging.*

BELOW: *A decorative plaque is made from a tile distressed to give it an aged look, then patterned with a noble looking black cock.*

Pollo Tonnato

— ❦ —

SERVINGS: 4 TO 6

This was one of my first chicken adaptations back in the early 1970s, when chicken mania was still in its infancy and it was considered unusual if not unorthodox to substitute chicken for other meats in a recipe. I secured the original recipe from a friendly waiter at Renato's restaurant, located in a section of New York City that was then considered the farther reaches of Greenwich Village and Little Italy, but today is part of the Soho sprawl. I remember enjoying my first taste of the traditional Italian *vitello tonnato*—veal in a smooth tuna sauce—on a summer's day in the restaurant's garden and thinking what a perfect dish it was for al fresco dining.

For this recipe the chicken breasts can be either poached or steamed. To give a suitable background flavor to the chicken, use diced celery, carrot, onion, and thyme in the poaching liquid or in the steamer basket. This dish is best made a day ahead and refrigerated, to allow the flavors of the sauce to marry with the chicken. Serve with a crisp field salad and rustic bread.

1 can (7 ounces) tuna in olive oil, preferably imported Italian

1 can (2 ounces) anchovy fillets, drained and rinsed

4 tablespoons salted capers, preserved in salt, soaked in water for 10 minutes and rinsed a few times (or capers preserved in vinegar, thoroughly rinsed and drained)

¾ to 1 cup olive oil

¼ cup freshly squeezed lemon juice

1 cup homemade mayonnaise (see page 159), or good-quality store-bought

2 pounds chicken breasts, poached or steamed (see page 125), chilled

Fresh basil, chopped

Caper berries or rinsed capers, for garnish

1 lemon, halved and thinly sliced (optional)

Sea salt

Freshly ground white pepper

Combine the tuna and anchovies in a bowl and pound into a paste.

Put the mixture in a food processor and add the capers. Blend while slowly pouring in ¾ cup oil. Add the lemon juice and blend, adding more oil if needed, until a creamy consistency is achieved.

Spoon the mayonnaise into a mixing bowl and stir in the tuna mixture; blend well.

Remove the chicken from the refrigerator and cut it into thin slices across the grain. Arrange the slices on a platter and spoon the sauce over the chicken.

Wrap tightly with plastic wrap and refrigerate overnight. Remove the chicken platter about 10 minutes before serving and garnish with basil and caper berries or capers; top each serving with a lemon slice.

Suggested Wine: Pinot Grigio

Collectors of pressed, molded, or blown glass may determine their preference and define their choices simply by color. In a home that is dominated by the color theme of blues and yellows set off against subtly different shades of whites, these cobalt blue-colored glass vases brimming with springtime bouquets and figurative chicken objects make a sparkling display.

FROM LEFT TO RIGHT: *The nesting hen is the motif for the covered candy dish, the egg cup, and the display dish for eggs. Proud roosters are the theme for the canister lid and the tall covered candy dish. Standing hens are the design for a pair of egg cups.*

Chicken Salads

—❦—

*F*or this recipe the chicken breasts can be poached or steamed. To give a suitable background flavor to the chicken, use diced celery, carrot, onion, and thyme in the poaching liquid or in the steamer basket.

My favorite store-bought sandwich from my days working in London came from the famous store Marks & Spencer. It was a brown wheat-bread sandwich filled with a curried chicken salad called "Coronation Chicken." The British connection to India has ensured the popularity of curry in England, but I was particularly curious about this dish's origins, with its titled and royal inferences. I assumed it went back to Queen Victoria, as English things so often do, so I consulted my *Mrs. Beaton's Household Management Book* from 1861, which did include a classic chicken curry but not this salad. Further enquiry led me to a much more contemporary aristocratic connection. The dish was devised by Constance Spry for a 1953 reception given at Westminster Hall in honor of Queen Elizabeth II's coronation.

Ms. Spry was considered the most popular cookery writer of that time and was asked to cater the reception, from food to flowers. Chicken salad mixed with rice, peas, and cucumber may seem a bit of a down-market dish for such an occasion and setting, but with war rationing not quite over and Westminster Hall's lack of cooking facilities, the ingredients needed to be simple and served cold.

Ms. Spry's recipe, published in *The Constance Spry Cookery Book* (1956), is far more involved than the one I use and, as did Marks & Spencer, I dispense with the rice salad she had included. Instead, I serve the salad on tasty grain bread or stuffed into whole-wheat pitas for quick lunches, or over a bed of delicate salad greens such as mâche (lamb's lettuce) for an elegant cold supper. My version, along with other chicken salads, follows.

When poaching chicken for salads, plain broth or stock will do, or compatible herbs and/or spices can be added.

Curried Chicken Salad

SERVINGS: 4 TO 6

1 teaspoon mild curry powder

1 cup homemade mayonnaise (see page 159) or good-quality store-bought

1 to 1½ tablespoons apricot butter or purée

2 teaspoons red wine vinegar

¾ cup chopped cucumber, peeled, seeded, and diced

½ cup finely sliced scallions

3 tablespoons finely chopped fresh cilantro or flat-leaf parsley

2 pounds chicken breasts, poached or steamed (see page 125), chilled and cubed

2 hard-boiled eggs, chopped

1½ tablespoons chopped pignoli

Mix the curry powder, mayonnaise, apricot butter, and vinegar in a large salad bowl. Blend thoroughly.

Add the remaining ingredients and toss together to coat the chicken and vegetables with the sauce.

Suggested Wine: Mâcon-Villages

---

*T*he hand-painted rooster-patterned tiles are from the famous Faienceries de Quimper of France.
CLOCKWISE FROM TOP LEFT: *Chicken, Cucumber, Scallion, and Watercress on panini; Asian Chicken Wrap; and Chicken, Prosciutto, and Tomato Pita.*

Chicken, Cucumber, Scallion & Watercress Sandwich

SERVINGS: 2 TO 3

2 tablespoons low-fat sour cream

Sea salt

Freshly ground pepper

2 teaspoons chopped fresh chives

2 pinches dried dill (optional)

1 cup coarsely chopped watercress leaves

1 to 1¼ cups peeled, seeded, and diced cucumber

¼ cup finely sliced scallions

¾ cup chilled and diced poached chicken breast (see page 125)

2 panini bread rolls, some of white center scooped out

In a salad or mixing bowl, combine the sour cream, salt and pepper to taste, chives, and dill; mix to combine.

Add the watercress and toss thoroughly. Add the cucumber and scallions and toss. Add the chicken and toss.

Spoon the mixture into the panini and serve.

Chicken, Prosciutto & Tomato Pita Sandwich

SERVINGS: 2

2 tablespoons olive oil

2 teaspoons freshly squeezed lemon juice

Sea salt

Freshly ground pepper

1 to 2 pinches of ground sage (optional)

1½ cups coarsely chopped red leaf lettuce

¾ to 1 cup chilled and diced poached chicken breast (see page 125)

2 slices prosciutto, shredded

½ cup diced fresh tomatoes

2 pita breads, tops cut off

In a salad or mixing bowl, combine the oil and lemon juice, and salt, pepper, and sage to taste; stir to blend.

Add the lettuce and toss thoroughly. Add the chicken and prosciutto and toss. Add the tomato and toss.

Spoon the mixture into the pita breads until brimming full and serve.

Chicken, Pimento & Mozzarella with Arugula Pita Sandwich

SERVINGS: 2

2 tablespoons olive oil

Sea salt

Freshly ground pepper

Pinch crumbled dried oregano

¾ cup coarsely chopped arugula

¾ cup chilled and diced poached chicken breast (see page 125)

⅓ cup (or 2 to 2½ ounces) fresh mozzarella, diced

⅓ cup coarsely chopped good-quality roasted pimento

2 pita breads, tops cut off

In a salad or mixing bowl, combine the oil, and salt, pepper, and oregano to taste; stir to blend.

Add the arugula and toss thoroughly. Add the chicken and mozzarella and toss. Add the pimentos and toss.

Spoon the mixture into the pita breads until brimming full and serve.

Chicken, Cucumber, Radish & Goat Cheese Pita Sandwich

SERVINGS: 2

2 tablespoons olive oil

Sea salt

Freshly ground pepper

1 to 2 pinches of dried ground thyme

1 cup coarsely chopped watercress leaves

3½ tablespoons diced radish

½ cup peeled, seeded, and diced cucumber

1½ ounces goat cheese, crumbled or diced

¾ cup chilled and diced poached chicken breast (see page 125)

2 pita breads, tops cut off

In a salad or mixing bowl, combine the oil, and salt, pepper, and thyme to taste; stir to blend.

Add the watercress, radish, and cucumber and toss thoroughly. Add the cheese and toss. Add the chicken and toss.

Spoon the mixture into the pita breads until brimming full and serve.

Asian Chicken Wrap

SERVINGS: 2

The inspiration for this comes from Peking duck, the classic Chinese dish that combines roasted duck with scallions, cucumbers, and hoisin sauce—all rolled up in a thin pancake.

  2 (8-inch) soft wheat tortillas

  About 4 tablespoons good-quality hoisin sauce

  2 leaves red leaf lettuce, trimmed from stems and halved

  1 whole chicken breast, poached (see page 125), at room temperature, shredded

  4 scallions, finely sliced lengthwise

  ½ medium cucumber, peeled, seeded, and cut into thin strips

Lay the tortillas on a cutting board, then spread some hoisin sauce over half of each one.

  Place a piece of lettuce over the sauce, then layer with chicken, scallions, and cucumbers, divided equally between the wraps. Roll up tightly.

Middle Eastern Chicken Wrap

SERVINGS: 2

  2 (8-inch) soft wheat tortillas

  2 to 3 chicken breast halves, poached (see page 125), chilled

  4 to 5 tablespoons good-quality hummus

  1 clove garlic, crushed through a garlic press

  4 leaves red leaf lettuce, trimmed from stems and halved

  3 to 4 tablespoons chopped fresh flat-leaf parsley

  3 scallions, finely chopped

Cut the chicken breasts into thin slices across the grain.

  In a mixing bowl, combine the hummus and garlic and blend together.

  Lay the wraps on a cutting board, and spread the hummus mixture over half of each one.

  Place a piece of lettuce over the hummus mixture, then layer with chicken, parsley, and scallions divided equally between the wraps. Roll up tightly.

Quimper is fine-grain earthenware fired with a tin-based glaze that takes its name from the town in Brittany, where it has been made since the seventeenth century. The traditional Quimper patterns are diverse, but perhaps the best known are the figures of Bretons in colorful traditional dress and the proud rooster in his position as the symbol of France. The site has been associated with the production of pottery as far back as Gallo-Roman times, and the rooster as national emblem has the same ancient connections.

ABOVE: The rooster motif dishes displayed on the eighteenth-century Irish dresser are created from the Quimper design archives and museum collection that represents 300 years of the factory's output. Like the tiles on the preceeding page, each plate is individually produced by hand and signed by the artisan with the factory mark and his initials.

5

✦

EGGS

I COULD NOT IMAGINE A CHICKEN COOKBOOK WITHOUT some recipes for eggs. Through both its meat and its eggs, the chicken provides the cook with the fixings for a wide variety of dishes—from appetizers and main courses to desserts. Like the chicken, the egg is very adaptable.

In their own right, eggs are a nutritional and inexpensive food that is relatively simple to prepare and quick to cook. They can be soft- or hard-boiled, coddled, poached, baked, or fried. Just blending the whites and yolks together creates scrambled eggs, omelets, and frittatas; separating the egg's elements leads to soufflés. The additions of flavorful spices, herbs, vegetables, or fruits turn the plain and simple egg into interesting dishes to serve from morning to midday to midnight. Eggs are a key ingredient in many successful sweet and savory sauces. They make custards, quiches, flans, and meringues what they are. Until recently, the consumption of raw eggs was recommended and even prescribed as a nutritional boost.

That the subject of eggs in recipes makes up the last chapter in this book is not my final word on which came first—the chicken or the egg. Some food historians feel they have the answer to this universal question, asserting that chicken precedes eggs in the world of cuisine. The argument goes that the cultivation and consumption of eggs developed only with the spread of poultry farming. When chickens roamed in the wild, their eggs were generally not eaten; this helped ensure their proliferation. In many cultures, the spiritual or religious symbolism of the egg—a representation of life, birth, and resurrection—precluded the eating of eggs.

Less subject to conjecture is which eggs came first, or how they were used. Early references to eggs appear in recipes that incorporate

American patchwork quilts represent a home craft elevated to the level of art—and rightly so. Amish quilts, for instance, are beautiful in their geometric simplicity and subtlety of color. More decorative, ornately patterned quilts and appliquéd coverlets can be feasts for the eyes as well, particularly quilts that interpret simple narratives, special events, or everyday occasions. Some quilts by contemporary artists, like this piece made from patterned scraps of fabrics, bring together the figurative and narrative traditions. This quilt, by Nancy Halpern, celebrates both the art of the quilt and that of the chicken.

them into other dishes, including some dating to ancient Greece. The ancient Romans often used eggs to bind sauces and in desserts. The creation of a baked custard made of eggs, milk, and honey is attributed to the Roman Apicius in 25 B.C. The omelet is a dish that also originated in Roman times, but scrambled eggs arrived much later, during the last half of the eighteenth century.

Historical references establish the egg as a food fit for kings. Clovis I, a king of the Franks during the early Middle Ages, was advised by his doctor to cut down on his eating of hard-boiled eggs as a remedy for his chronic indigestion. In the ninth century, Charlemagne issued orders to ensure that his farms were well stocked with poultry and their eggs. Louis the XIV adored meringue. Louis XV is said to have eaten hard-boiled eggs every Sunday; supposedly he was so adept at peeling them that people came to court to watch him. To maintain a steady supply of good fresh eggs, the king kept his own laying hens in the attics of his palace at Versailles; the best of these accompanied him on his travels.

During the fifteenth century, Caterina Sforza, the daughter of the Duke of Milan, was held prisoner in Rome by the Borgia family. She was given little to eat, feared being poisoned, and would have starved if it weren't for a devoted monk who smuggled Caterina enough eggs to sustain her until she was freed by the French.

By the sixteenth century, the egg was well established in its many cooked forms as part of the everyday diet and it has remained so since. The following recipes are a modest sampling of the different types of dishes that eggs can provide.

Scrambled Eggs with Ricotta & Cherry Tomatoes

Scrambled Eggs with Anchovies on Whole-Grain Bread Toasts

Omelet with Smoked Salmon, Sour Cream & Salmon Caviar

Egg-White Omelet with Mushrooms & Shallots

Leek & Cheese Omelet

Chile & Cheese Frittata

Ham, Peas, Potato & Onion Frittata

Poached Eggs & Sautéed Chicken Livers with Wilted Spinach Salad

Sweet French Croissant Toasts with Sautéed Apples

Monterey Jack French Toasts

French Cheese French Toasts

English Breakfast

Hard-Boiled Eggs: Stuffed & Chopped

Quiche Lorraine à Béatrice

Mayonnaise

Scrambled Eggs with Ricotta & Cherry Tomatoes

SERVINGS: 4

In England, they are mumbled, in France *brouillés*, and over here, scrambled. Wherever they are, they are very likely the most popular of cooked eggs.

This dish is equally good without the bacon, or substitute turkey bacon for a meal with less fat.

4 slices thick-cut bacon, cut into 1-inch
   strips (optional)
8 large eggs
¾ cup ricotta
½ teaspoon sea salt
Freshly ground white pepper
4 tablespoons chopped fresh basil
1 to 2 tablespoons unsalted butter
6 ounces sweet cherry tomatoes, halved
   or quartered depending on size
   (about 1 cup)

Cook the bacon in a skillet until brown and crisp. Drain on paper towels and set aside.

Combine the eggs, ricotta, salt, white pepper, and half the basil in a mixing bowl, and whisk to a light and fluffy consistency.

Heat the butter in another skillet. Pour in the egg mixture. Gently cook over medium heat, stirring and tilting the pan to distribute the eggs. Gently stir in the tomatoes and bacon. Continue stirring and pushing until the eggs form soft mounds. Immediately remove the pan from the heat.

Sprinkle with the remaining basil and serve.

From the ninth century on, the form of the cock was used for weathervanes mounted on church steeples, to be seen as a symbol of vigilance against evil, an emblem of spiritual awakening, and a call to worship.

Weathervanes were first imported to the Colonies in the seventeenth century, but by the eighteenth century the American weathervane and its maker were elevated to positions of art form and artist. The weathercock was a popular feature on shops and private homes in both Europe and America, and in time became a symbol of early American village life.

Cock designs for weathervanes achieved their height of popularity in the mid-eighteenth century, but by the mid-nineteenth century the more ornate style of new Victorian houses made the cock seem a less than suitable motif. Its popularity waned and the weathercock was relegated to the tops of more rustic structures such as barns and outbuildings.

The cock remained a popular figure for weathervane designs until the latter part of the nineteenth century, although its significance as a religious symbol had diminished.

The crossbreeding of English Cornish chickens with Mediterranean fowl in America accounts for the very different look of weathercocks in the United States, compared to those in Britain or France. The result was a rooster with an elegant shape accentuated by the high arched tail feathers as shown in the weathercocks here.

LEFT: *The New England weathercock at left was cast in iron and dates from the nineteenth century.*

OPPOSITE: *The cock fashioned in sheet iron also dates from the nineteenth century and sits on a new base that creates the effect of a picket fence.*

Scrambled Eggs with Anchovies on Whole-Grain Bread Toasts

SERVINGS: 4

Perhaps due to the extremes of their effects on the palate—salty and sharp contrasted with soft and rich—anchovies and eggs have a natural affinity that is exploited in numerous dishes. A mixed green salad with a vinaigrette dressing is a good accompaniment.

5 large eggs

3 to 4 tablespoons crème fraîche or sour cream

Freshly ground pepper

1 tablespoon Worcestershire sauce

Hot red pepper sauce

1 to 2 tablespoons unsalted butter

8 to 10 canned anchovy fillets, drained, rinsed, and cut in half lengthwise

1 tablespoon plus 1 teaspoon finely chopped fresh cilantro or flat-leaf parsley

4 (½-inch-thick) slices mixed-grain bread, lightly toasted (and buttered while hot—optional)

Combine the eggs, crème fraîche, pepper, Worcestershire sauce, and a dash or two of hot sauce in a mixing bowl, and whisk to a light and fluffy consistency.

Heat the butter in a skillet. Pour in the egg mixture. Gently cook over medium heat, stirring and tilting the pan to distribute the eggs. Continue stirring and pushing until the eggs form soft mounds. Immediately remove the pan from the heat.

Place a slice of toasted bread on individual plates. Spoon equal portions of the eggs onto each. Arrange anchovy pieces on the eggs and sprinkle with the cilantro.

The notion of royal eggs developed out of Lenten tradition in France from the ninth century on and reached a high point during the reign of Louis XIV. But the most famous of royal eggs are surely those made by Peter Carl Fabergé from about 1884 to 1916 for the last czars of Russia, Alexander III and Nicholas II. They are of unquestionable beauty and among the finest examples of enamel work ever executed.

The eggs were commissioned by the Imperial family in the Russian tradition of exchanging decorated eggs with family members and friends at Easter. They were remarkable for the intricacy of design—fashioned in precious metals, fabulously colored in enamel and often lavishly embellished with jewels. The eggs, which often took two or more years to create, when opened revealed interiors as elaborate as the exteriors. Aside from Easter itself, the eggs commemorated important and historic events.

BELOW: The materials combined in this design are gold, enamel, diamonds, rubies, and suede. The egg was given by Aleksandr Ferdinandovich Kelch to his wife in 1898 and, according to one expert, is thought to be a "more elaborate conceptualization of Fabergé's design for the first imperial egg." The portraits of Nicholas II and that of the czarevitch on the easel were added to the egg at a later date.

Omelet with Smoked Salmon, Sour Cream & Salmon Caviar

SERVINGS: 4

This is how we enjoy the typical Sunday brunch of bagels, smoked salmon, and cream cheese—in a lighter way. This omelet also makes an elegant dish to serve as a midnight or after-theater supper, accompanied by champagne and followed by a dessert soufflé.

Depending on the size of your pan, cook four individual omelettes or two larger ones that can be divided in half for serving.

8 large eggs
Sea salt
Freshly ground white pepper
1 to 2 tablespoons unsalted butter
    or vegetable oil
6 ounces smoked salmon, cut into
    short strips
4 tablespoons minced scallions
4 tablespoons low-fat sour cream
4 tablespoons salmon caviar

Lightly beat the eggs, salt, and white pepper in a mixing bowl until just combined.

Heat the butter or lightly wipe a nonstick pan with just a bit of oil. To make 2 large omelets, pour half of the egg mixture into the pan and tilt it so the eggs run evenly over the surface. As they set, distribute half of the salmon and scallions over the surface. Slide the omelet in the pan so that one third of it folds over the filling. Shake and slide to fold the rest of the omelet over, turning it at the same time out onto a warm plate and keep warm. Repeat with the remaining ingredients.

Divide the double omelets in half. Serve each portion with 1 tablespoon each of sour cream and salmon caviar.

Suggested Wine: Dry champagne

At nearly 13 inches in height when opened, this elaborate clock is the largest Fabergé Easter egg known today. The vivid blue enamel is banded in gold and ornamented with diamonds and pearls. A gold grille at the top opens to reveal an enameled rooster that bobs its head and flaps its wings "to crow the hour." The egg is believed to have been presented by Czar Nicholas II to his mother, the Dowager Empress Maria Feodorovna and dates from 1903.

Egg-White Omelet with Mushrooms & Shallots

SERVINGS: 4

Make this as two omelets, each to be divided. Serve with sautéed spinach or crisp or wilted spinach salad for a perfect brunch, lunch, or supper.

2 tablespoons olive oil

3 tablespoons chopped shallots

1 tablespoon Marsala

½ pound shiitake or cremini mushrooms, chopped

3 tablespoons finely chopped fresh flat-leaf parsley

12 egg whites

Sea salt

Freshly ground white pepper

Preheat the oven to 450 degrees, setting the rack at the middle level.

Heat 1 tablespoon of the oil in a sauté pan over medium heat. Add the shallots and gently sweat them for 2 minutes. Add the Marsala, cook 1 minute, stirring, then add the mushrooms. Cook for 5 to 8 minutes; stir in the parsley, set aside, and keep warm.

Whisk the egg whites and the salt and white pepper together in a mixing bowl until soft peaks form.

Heat 1½ teaspoons oil in a nonstick ovenproof sauté pan, tilting it to coat the bottom and sides. Pour in half the egg-white mixture, put the pan in the oven, and bake until the eggs are set, about 6 minutes. Slide the omelet out of the pan onto a warmed plate. Repeat for the second omelette.

Divide each omelet in half and serve on warmed plates; top with equal portions of the mushroom mixture.

Suggested Wine: California Vin Gris

Cardboard egg boxes decorated with elaborate designs focusing on images of hens, roosters and chicks are of German origin and date from 1910–1930; the whimsical illustrations of chickens as a bridal couple and with umbrellas are dated slightly earlier, 1900–1910. The boxes would have held candy or other Easter treats and sweets. The tin container, right, features a hen and her chicks on one side, the rooster on the other, and is also from 1900–1910.

Leek & Cheese Omelet

SERVINGS: 2

*I*t was not until I moved to England that I learned to truly appreciate leeks and cheese together, a wildly popular combination there for quiches and omelets.

4 or 5 large eggs
1 tablespoon low-fat sour cream
½ cup Shropshire blue cheese or sharp
   cheddar, crumbled
Salt
Freshly ground pepper
1½ tablespoons unsalted butter

½ cup thinly sliced leeks, carefully
   washed
1 scallion, thinly sliced
1 tablespoon chopped fresh chive

Lightly beat the eggs and sour cream together in a mixing bowl, stir in the cheese, and season with salt and pepper.

Melt the butter in an omelet pan or skillet. Add the leeks and gently cook until they are translucent and tender.

Pour the eggs into the pan and tilt it so the eggs run evenly over the bottom. As the eggs set, sprinkle the scallion and chives over.

Tilt the pan on a slight angle and slide the omelet to fold one third of it over. Shake and slide to fold it over again and roll it out onto a warm plate. Cut the omelet in half to serve.

Suggested Wine: Saumur Rouge

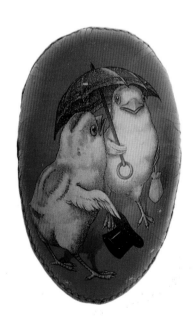

Chile & Cheese Frittata

SERVINGS: 4

A frittata can be cooked on the stovetop or in the oven. In the first method, the frittata is cooked until the eggs are set on the bottom, turned onto a plate, then slipped back into the pan to finish cooking. Or, a stovetop frittata can be placed under the broiler for a few minutes once the bottom is set; this avoids the slightly tricky flipping. Either way, a golden top will be achieved. You must use an oven-proof skillet if you put the frittata under the broiler.

To bake a frittata following the method described below, use any ovenproof baking dish, an ovenproof skillet, or individual gratin dishes or ramekins. For cooking individual portions with the stovetop method, there are special pans made with portion-sized wells. Since the sizes of the wells and gratin dishes vary somewhat, the amount given here may be a bit more than you need.

6 large eggs, beaten

2 tablespoons low-fat sour cream

Sea salt

Freshly ground pepper

½ cup mixed shredded cheese, such as Monterey Jack, cheddar, queso, and asadero (such blends can be purchased already shredded)

1 tablespoon unsalted butter, plus additional for the pan

1 scallion, finely chopped

4 ounces canned mild green chiles, diced

2 to 3 tablespoons finely chopped fresh cilantro

Mix the eggs with the sour cream in a bowl, season with salt and pepper. Stir in half the cheeses; set aside.

Heat the butter in a small skillet and cook the scallions for 1 minute. Add the chiles and cook to heat through; set aside.

Preheat the broiler.

Grease the wells of the frittata pan with butter. Divide the chile mixture among the wells and then pour equal amounts of the egg mixture into each well. Cook over low heat until the eggs have set and the edges are lightly browned.

Sprinkle the tops with the remaining cheese and place the pan under the broiler until the tops are golden brown (see Note). Turn out onto a large platter and keep warm while you finish the rest.

Note: If you are not using an ovenproof pan, first turn the frittatas out of the pan onto a small baking sheet, carefully turn them right-side up, and place them under the broiler.

Suggested Beverage: Margaritas or white Malbec

LEFT: *This generously proportioned earthenware serving bowl features a painterly rooster at its center. It is the work of Ron Meyers, one of a growing number of contemporary potters who produce one-of-a-kind pieces.*

OPPOSITE: *The kitchen of a chicken collector and cook is bound to be well appointed with chicken objects and paraphernalia. A brunch of Chile & Cheese Frittatas waits in a special pan for making individual frittatas surrounded by pottery, table linen, a pot-holder, and even a treasured painting by a young member of the family—all featuring chick, hen, and rooster motifs*

This religious totem, said to be a shrine sculpture of the Yoruba of Nigeria, is carved in wood and painted. A nesting hen tops a base that contains another nesting hen and human figures within. It could well reflect the belief in the protective and nurturing qualities attributed to the hen.

Ham, Peas, Potato & Onion Frittata

SERVINGS: 4

*H*ere the frittatas are oven-baked as individual portions in 7-inch-diameter by 1½-inch-deep gratin dishes. The combination of ingredients for the filling of this frittata is a traditional one used in many other dishes—quiches, savory pies, omelets—and invariably is referred to as "country style."

2 tablespoons unsalted butter, plus
   additional for the baking dishes
1 large potato, peeled and cubed
Sea salt
Freshly ground pepper
4 to 5 ounces slab bacon, cut into
   lardons (see page 90)
4 tablespoons chopped onion
6 large eggs, beaten
2 tablespoons sour cream
½ cup canned petits pois (young peas),
   drained, washed, and drained again

Preheat the oven to 350 degrees, setting the rack at the middle level.

Lightly coat 4 individual gratin dishes with some of the butter and set them aside.

Put the potato in a saucepan of cold water and bring to a boil over high heat. Cook for 8 minutes or until tender, drain, season with salt and pepper, and set aside.

Heat 1 tablespoon of the butter in a skillet and cook the bacon until golden brown and crisp. Remove the bacon with a slotted spoon and set it on paper towels to drain.

Add the onion to the pan and sauté until still soft and golden brown. Remove the onions with a slotted spoon and set aside.

Add the potato to the pan and sauté, stirring, until lightly browned. Add the potatoes to the onions.

Combine the eggs with the sour cream, season with salt and pepper to taste, and whisk until frothy; set aside.

Divide the bacon, *petits pois*, potatoes, and onions among the buttered gratin dishes. Carefully pour in the egg mixture, place the gratins in the oven, and bake for 20 minutes or until set.

Serve the frittatas in their dishes.

Suggested Wine: White from Savoie

Poached Eggs & Sautéed Chicken Livers with Wilted Spinach Salad

SERVINGS: 2

A variation on the American classic spinach salad and the French frisée salad that combines elements of the two. This is served warm or at room temperature with a traditional vinaigrette dressing. The quantity of dressing given here is more than needed for this dish.

For the dressing

⅓ cup white wine vinegar

⅔ cup olive oil

1½ tablespoons Dijon mustard

Sea salt

Freshly ground pepper

For the salad

1 cup cauliflower florets

2 strips thick-cut bacon, cut into
  1-inch pieces

1 tablespoon peanut or corn oil

1 cup sliced cremini mushrooms or white
  button or shiitake tops

4 scallions, including tender green tops,
  cut lengthwise into quarters

6 ounces sweet cherry tomatoes (about
  1 cup)

10 ounces chicken livers

1½ pounds baby leaf spinach

2 large eggs

Salt

Freshly ground pepper

Whisk the ingredients for the dressing together, in order, in a measuring cup.

In a saucepan of boiling water, blanch the cauliflower for 3 minutes, then drain and set aside.

Sauté the bacon in a medium-sized skillet or nonstick sauté pan. Set aside on a paper towel to drain.

Return the pan to high heat, add some of the oil if needed, and quickly sauté the mushrooms for 3 minutes.

Add the scallions and tomatoes to the skillet and cook, shaking the pan, for 5 minutes. Transfer the vegetables to a bowl.

Heat the remaining oil in the skillet and sauté the chicken livers for 4 to 5 minutes, until they are nicely browned all over and cooked through. Remove from the skillet with a slotted spoon and set aside.

Meanwhile, bring 2 to 3 inches of water to boil in a large, wide saucepan and lower the heat to medium to maintain a simmer.

Add the spinach to the skillet and quickly sauté for about 2 minutes or until just wilted, then drain thoroughly, pressing with the back of a spoon to squeeze out any liquid.

Pour some of the vinaigrette dressing into a salad bowl, add the spinach, and toss to coat it thoroughly; divide between individual serving plates. (Reserve the leftover dressing for another use.) Divide the sautéed vegetables, bacon, and chicken livers between the plates and keep them warm in the oven.

Break one egg into a small heatproof bowl, lower the bowl into the simmering water of the saucepan so that one edge of the bowl is just submerged, and then gently slide the egg into the water. Repeat for the second egg, being careful not to let the eggs touch.

Cover the pan and poach at a simmer until the egg whites are opaque and to your timing preference. Remove the eggs with a slotted spoon and drain them over paper towels. Serve the eggs on top of the dressed salad. Season with salt and pepper.

Sweet French Croissant Toasts with Sautéed Apples

SERVINGS: 4

*P*ain *perdu* translates literally as "lost bread," perhaps referring to the dish's original purpose as a second use for day-old bread. You can use day-old or freshly baked breads or rolls of almost any description and serve the toasts with all sorts of sweet toppings—from maple syrup to jams or cooked or fresh fruits.

3 to 4 tablespoons unsalted butter

2 tart apples, peeled, cored, and sliced

3 large eggs

2 tablespoons heavy cream

2 teaspoons sugar

4 day-old croissants, sliced in half crosswise

Ground cinnamon

Maple syrup

Preheat the oven to 180 degrees.

Heat 2 tablespoons of the butter in a sauté pan. Sauté the apples until just tender. Transfer them to an ovenproof dish and keep warm in the oven.

Beat the eggs, cream, and sugar in a shallow bowl large enough to hold the croissants a piece or two at a time. Dip the slices in the mixture and soak thoroughly.

Heat the remaining butter in a skillet, add the croissants, and sauté for 3 minutes on each side or until golden.

Serve the French toasts topped with the apples; sprinkle with cinnamon, and offer the maple syrup at the table.

Monterey Jack French Toasts

SERVINGS: 4

In our house we enjoy savory French toasts coated with a variety of cheeses instead of the traditional grilled cheese sandwich. I often add grilled onions, roasted tomatoes, or asparagus to make a full meal. A variety of toppings—from mustards to chutneys to salsas—are great-tasting accompaniments. You can serve your favorite salsa with this version with great success.

3 large eggs

2 tablespoons buttermilk (or whole milk)

¾ teaspoon salt

4 (½-inch-thick) slices challah or potato bread

½ cup shredded Monterey Jack with jalapeño cheese, or packaged mixed shredded cheese labeled "Mexican," "Tex-Mex," or similar

2 to 3 tablespoons unsalted butter

Beat the eggs, buttermilk, and salt in a shallow bowl large enough to hold the bread slices a piece or two at a time. Dip and soak the slices in the mixture.

Heat the butter in a skillet. Just prior to cooking, sprinkle one side of each slice with a heaping tablespoon of cheese.

Gently place the slices, cheese side down, in the pan, taking care not to let the cheese drop off. Sprinkle the top side of each slice with another heaping table-spoon of cheese. Fry for about 3 minutes, turn carefully, and fry the other side.

Chicken charm was a prevailing decorative theme for the home during the second half of the twentieth century, mass-marketed to country, suburban, and city folks across America. Now genuinely collectible and nearly antique, these nouveau kitsch tea towels are a perfect example.

French Cheese French Toasts

SERVINGS: 4

The cheese used for the coatings can vary, as long as it can be shredded. You can shred the cheese yourself or select from the large variety of different types and flavor combinations that are available, already shredded, in the dairy refrigerator section of your supermarket.

3 large eggs

1½ tablespoons buttermilk (or whole milk)

¾ teaspoon salt

2 teaspoons white wine Worcestershire sauce

4 (½-inch-thick) slices of sourdough bread

½ cup shredded Comté or Gruyère cheese

2 to 3 tablespoons unsalted butter

Beat the eggs, buttermilk, salt, and Worcestershire sauce in a shallow bowl large enough to hold the bread slices a piece or two at a time. Dip and soak the slices in the mixture.

Heat the butter in a skillet. Just prior to cooking, sprinkle one side of each slice with a heaping tablespoon of cheese.

Gently place the slices, cheese side down, in the pan, taking care not to let the cheese drop off. Sprinkle the top sides with cheese. Fry for about 3 minutes, turn carefully, and fry the other sides.

The symbol of the egg and, of course, the chicken are at the heart of Easter traditions. However, the ornamental and decorated Easter eggs enjoyed by Christians each year are the legacy of a variety of cultural traditions.

In ancient China, Greece, and Rome eggs were offered as gifts celebrating spring or love. In the British Isles, colored eggs honored pagan deities. Decorated eggs helped mark springtime and, later, Easter in central Europe.

The most familiar of these are probably the richly decorated traditional Ukranian and Russian Easter eggs, available as two types. Krashanky, hard-boiled eggs dyed a solid color, are often blessed and eaten as part of ritual. Sharing krashanky with family expresses unity and hope for a happy year ahead. Pysanky, from the word "to write," are raw eggs dyed and decorated in fine detail. Today, design motifs combine both Christian symbols and simple geometric patterns from pagan times, when eggs—their yolks representing the sun—were used in sun worship ceremonies.

Other European traditions expressing the more secular side of Easter were quickly adopted in America as well. The Easter bunny, the egg hunt, and the egg-rolling contest on the White House lawn are all offspring of older traditions. And the hen, rooster, and chick are featured in many decorative objects this time of year.

Witness the basket, opposite, brimming with Easter treats, including chocolate, sugar, candy-coated, or fancy wrapped confectionary eggs—not to mention the egg-shaped jelly bean. In the form of sweets, toys, or even baby booties, the baby chick theme always proves irresistible.

English Breakfast

SERVINGS: 2

A breakfast treat we always enjoyed when traveling around the English countryside was a traditional "cooked breakfast." A hearty start to the day, English breakfast includes a selection of mostly fried elements—eggs, bacon, pork sausages, tomatoes, mushroom caps, and sometimes even fried bread. At home we have adapted this to make it something a bit lighter—substituting turkey bacon and chicken sausage and grilling rather than frying.

Tea, thick-cut orange marmalade, and HP Sauce—an unusual-flavored piquant brown sauce that can be found at some specialty shops and better supermarkets—complete our English breakfast.

2 chicken sausages, plain or seasoned
  with herbs

2 large mushroom caps (3 to 4 ounces each)

2 to 4 slices turkey bacon

1 large tomato (about ½ pound),
  thickly sliced

3 or 4 eggs

2 thick slices whole-grain wheat or
  country white bread

1 to 2 tablespoons chopped fresh
  flat-leaf parsley

Preheat the grill or a nonstick grill pan. Cook the sausages for 10 to 15 minutes. Add the mushroom caps and cook for 5 to 8 additional minutes. Add the bacon strips and tomatoes and continue cooking for 8 to 10 minutes.

While the meat and vegetables are finishing, heat a nonstick sauté pan over medium heat, fry the eggs to your liking, and toast the bread.

OPPOSITE: *When the English are about to take tea, they often ask "Who'll be mother?" meaning, who will pour and serve? Given this convention, what could be more appropriate than a tea cozy fashioned as a nesting mother hen. Designed to keep the contents of a teapot warm, tea cozies are famous for their fanciful figurative shapes and decorative embellishments. Tea cozies reached the height of their popularity before WWII.*

This hen-shaped tea cozy, from the late 1940s or early 1950s, is no exception. Cut from wool, it is generously detailed with crewelwork, padded, and lined with satin. The late-nineteenth-century Dresden china tea cup, sweetly decorated with chicks, and a new linen tea towel completes the setting.

RIGHT: *The rooster was a beloved character in the late-nineteenth-century merry-go-round menagerie, but very expensive to produce. Ornately designed and intricately carved, this American carousel figure was the work of the renowned Gustav Dentzel. Dentzel's work ceased to be produced after 1900 and only five of his chickens are thought to exist today. This one was fitted with a saddle seat for riders. In spite of his glamour and popularity, the rooster was rarely positioned in the prestigious outer row, which was mainly inhabited by horses.*

Hard-Boiled Eggs: Stuffed & Chopped

Boiled eggs should not be boiled for the whole cooking time, as it produces tough and rubbery eggs. For the best results, place room-temperature eggs in a saucepan and fill the pan with enough cold water to cover by an inch or so. Bring the water to a boil over medium-high heat and immediately turn off the heat. Cover the pan and let stand for 12 to 15 minutes, depending on the size of the eggs. Remove the eggs from the pan and transfer them to a bowl of cold water. When the eggs have cooled, in about 3 minutes, remove them from the water and peel.

As part of an hors d'oeuvres selection or at a picnic, stuffed eggs are wildly popular. Here are a few variations.

Stuffed Eggs

3 hard-boiled eggs (per above), peeled, halved, and yolks removed and reserved

Chive Mustard

1½ teaspoons chopped fresh chives
2 teaspoons Dijon mustard
1 teaspoon low-fat sour cream
Pinch of sea salt
Freshly ground pepper

Horseradish & Sour Cream

2 teaspoons prepared horseradish
1 teaspoon low-fat sour cream
Freshly ground pepper

Tarragon, Paprika & Mayonnaise

2 teaspoons finely chopped fresh tarragon
1 tablespoon plus 1 teaspoon homemade mayonnaise (see page 159), or good-quality store-bought
1 to 2 pinches paprika
Pinch of sea salt
Freshly ground pepper

Olive & Mayonnaise

2 teaspoons prepared black olive tapenade
1 teaspoon homemade mayonnaise (see page 159), or good-quality store-bought
Freshly ground pepper

Cilantro, Curry & Mayonnaise or Yogurt

1 teaspoon finely chopped fresh cilantro
1 teaspoon mild curry powder
1 tablespoon plus 1 teaspoon homemade mayonnaise (see page 159), or good-quality store-bought, or plain yogurt
Pinch of sea salt
Freshly ground pepper

Parsley, Anchovy & Mayonnaise

1 teaspoon finely chopped fresh flat-leaf parsley
1 to 2 teaspoons chopped anchovy fillets
¼ teaspoon granulated garlic
2 teaspoons homemade mayonnaise (see page 159), or good-quality store-bought
Freshly ground pepper

Mix the yolks with the ingredients of your choice in a small bowl and blend to a paste. Spoon the mixture onto the egg-white halves.

Note: If you want very full stuffed eggs, cook one extra for each three and add the extra yolk to the filling.

Chopped Eggs

Anchovy & Caper Chopped Hard-Boiled Eggs

I usually serve this egg salad as a spread, presenting it in a bowl along with squares of toasted breads with their crusts removed.

> 6 hard-boiled eggs (see page 156), peeled
>
> 1 2-ounce can anchovy fillets, drained, washed, and drained again, then coarsely chopped
>
> 2 tablespoons salted capers, washed, soaked, washed, and drained again, then coarsely chopped
>
> 1 tablespoon finely chopped fresh flat-leaf parsley
>
> 1 tablespoon plus 1 teaspoon homemade mayonnaise (see page 159) or good-quality store-bought

Chop the eggs and set them aside.

Combine the anchovies, capers, parsley, and mayonnaise in a medium-sized bowl.

Add the eggs and stir to combine.

Chopped Eggs with Smoked Salmon, Caviar & Scallions

This is good served on thinly sliced brown bread cut into triangles or on Scottish oat cakes.

> 6 hard-boiled eggs (see page 156), peeled
>
> 6 ounces smoked salmon, coarsely chopped
>
> 4 tablespoons chopped scallions
>
> 1 tablespoon finely chopped fresh dill
>
> 2 tablespoons low-fat sour cream
>
> 4 ounces salmon caviar

Chop the eggs and set them aside.

Combine the salmon, scallions, dill, and sour cream in a medium-sized bowl.

Add the eggs and stir to combine. Gently fold in the salmon caviar.

This antique rooster dish, made specifically for stuffed eggs, makes an amusing presentation at cocktail time. Here it is surrounded with other old and new chicken collectibles, including a pair of china salt and pepper shakers (a rooster and a hen, of course); a large ceramic cock figurine from the late 1940s or early 1950s; and a turn of the (twentieth) century barnyard painting as a backdrop.

Quiche Lorraine à Béatrice

—🐓—

SERVINGS: 6 TO 8

For my husband there is no better (or other) quiche than the one his sister, Béatrice, makes. This is her recipe. It is especially good served with a salad of steamed broccoli and cherry tomatoes in a simple vinaigrette.

This recipe requires a 9-inch quiche mold. If you are pastry-phobic, a good-quality store-bought shell can be used.

Corrugated metal emphasizes the abstract style of this chicken painting by the famous Outsider artist Jimmy Sudduth.

2⅓ cups all-purpose flour, sifted

½ teaspoon salt

10 tablespoons unsalted butter, plus additional for the quiche mold

½ cup ice water

2 tablespoons unsalted butter

2 medium onions, peeled and thinly sliced

½ pound slab bacon, cut into 1-inch squares

Freshly ground pepper

7 eggs

1⅓ cup whole milk

½ cup heavy cream

All-purpose flour

Place the flour and salt in a bowl and stir to combine. Cut 8 tablespoons of the butter into small pieces and, using a fork, pastry cutter, or your fingers, work the butter into the dry mixture until it has the texture of very coarse meal; there should be no large discernible pieces of butter in the mixture.

Pour some of the ice water into the mixture, and, working quickly, mix just to combine. Add water as necessary, removing any dough that holds together. Sprinkle the remaining mixture lightly with water and gather it together. Pat all the dough into a thick disk, dust it with flour, wrap it in plastic or waxed paper, and put it in the refrigerator.

Preheat the oven to 375 degrees.

Heat the remaining butter in a skillet; add the onions and gently cook them until soft and golden, but do not let them brown. Remove the onions from the pan with a slotted spoon and set aside.

Add the bacon to the pan and cook until golden brown; combine the bacon and onions and season to taste with pepper. Set aside to cool to room temperature.

Whisk the eggs in a bowl; add the milk and cream and whisk to combine.

Butter and lightly flour a 9-inch quiche mold.

Place the dough on a lightly floured board and roll it into an 11-inch circle. Carefully fit the dough into the prepared pan, folding any excess in around the edge.

Spread the onion and bacon mixture into the bottom of the shell. Pour the egg mixture carefully over the onion and bacon in the shell.

Bake for 45 minutes or until the custard is set but not dry—it should still tremble a bit at the center when moved.

Suggested Wine: Light red, such as Meursault

Mayonnaise

MAKES 1½ CUPS

This is the way my husband Michel's mother taught him to make a mayonnaise, and it is the method we always follow. He claims that the success of this recipe requires three things: the best-quality oils, the freshest eggs, and a wooden spoon.

Use this recipe for the mayonnaise in the mayonnaise-based sauces in this book. The exception is the aïoli sauce (page 129), in which the mustard is omitted and a garlic paste is incorporated (a boiled potato may be added as a thickener).

1½ tablespoons Dijon mustard
1 egg yolk from a large egg,
    at room temperature
½ teaspoon salt
¼ teaspoon freshly ground pepper
1½ cups oil (see Note)
1 tablespoon freshly squeezed
    lemon juice

Put the egg yolk in a medium-sized bowl and stir in the salt and pepper. Blend in the mustard. When smooth, very slowly and gradually pour in the oil in a thin but steady stream while stirring vigorously with a wooden spoon. As the eggs and oil begin to thicken—the oil forms an emulsion with the egg—you can increase the flow of the oil slightly. Continue until almost all the oil is used, then stir in the lemon juice. Finish with the remaining oil and stir. (The wooden spoon should stand upright on its own in the center the bowl when the mayonnaise is done.)

Note: You can use a combination of any two good-quality oils, or just one, for the total of 1½ cups. We traditionally use equal parts of first-cold-press extra-virgin olive oil with a fine-quality vegetable or corn oil. We also make sure to have a very fresh free-range egg.

The standing wire basket with individual spiral cups to hold eggs securely is an old-fashioned storage system that kept eggs safe from cracking or breaking. In the days before refrigeration was in wide use, it could be set in a pantry or cold room where eggs stayed fresh. French cafés and bars are still known for having hard-boiled eggs readily available in baskets like these. But these days, wire egg baskets are most often used to display decorative eggs made from stone, wood, or porcelain.

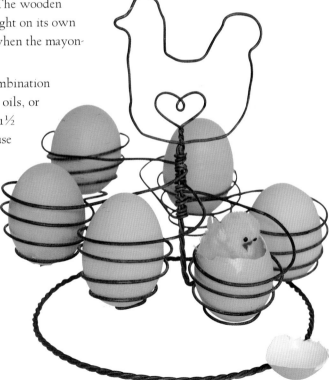

APPENDIX

Chicken Safety Basics

I MOST OFTEN PURCHASE MY CHICKENS FROM A few butchers whom I know well, and where I never have any doubts about the quality or freshness of the product. I also buy chicken from a supermarket that does a brisk business in poultry both from its butcher department or already packaged from the refrigerated meats and poultry section. In general I prefer chicken that is grain-fed, free of chemicals and antibiotics and was not caged, but left free to roam, but I admit to using mass-produced poultry in a pinch. I apply the same standard for eggs.

When purchasing packaged chicken be aware of "sell-by" dates whenever they are provided and avoid chicken in damaged packages. Place your poultry purchases in separate plastic bags for the trip home, to keep them away from the other groceries. Always check eggs for any sign of cracks in the shell no matter how slight, and never purchase or use from your refrigerator damaged eggs as they may have become contaminated.

Once home, wash the chicken in cold water, trim off any unwanted tissue, sinew or fat, remove innards, pat dry and wrap in plastic wrap or place in a plastic bag or covered dish. Chicken keeps well for up to two days in the refrigerator and three to four months in the freezer (although freezing will result in some loss of taste and texture in the cooked dish).

Practicing good hygiene in the kitchen when handling and preparing chicken and thorough cooking are the sensible and best protection against food-borne diseases like salmonella.

Here are some simple rules to follow.

- Be sure to keep your hands and nails and all work surfaces and utensils scrubbed clean. Wash up before and after, but also during preparations so that raw chicken does not come into contact with cooked foods or those to be eaten raw. This also applies to any dish that has been in contact with the raw chicken you are preparing. Wash the dish before returning cooked chicken to it.

- Discard the marinades used for a chicken dish, unless it is thoroughly cooked.

- Frozen chicken should be thawed in the refrigerator or microwave oven and never left out to thaw at room temperature.

- All chicken, whether whole or in parts, should be cooked thoroughly. Whole chicken is considered cooked when it reaches an internal temperature of 180 degrees on a meat thermometer; boneless parts when they register 160 degrees. Doneness also can be judged by piercing the chicken with a fork or knife point at its thickest point, and considered cooked when the juices run clear and without any trace of pink.

- Cook a dish all the way through without interruption, do not let the chicken stand until it is cooked through.

- Chicken must not be cooked at temperatures below 325 degrees.

- Cooked chicken should not be served at temperatures between 40 degrees and 140 degrees, which are the most opportune for the growth of harmful bacteria.

- Cooked chicken should be refrigerated or frozen no longer than 2 hours after finishing or serving, and as soon as 1 hour if the weather is hot.

- Discard any raw or cooked chicken if there is a doubt about its condition.

Smoke Points of some cooking fats/oils:

Lard	361-401 degrees
vegetable shortening	356-370 degrees
vegetable oils	445-450 degrees
Peanut, Safflower, Soybean	450 degrees
Grape seed	445 degrees
Canola	435 degrees
Corn, Olive, Sesame	410 degrees
Sunflower	390 degrees

Bibliography

American Country Folk Art. Virginia: Time Life Books, 1990.

Bishop, Robert, *All Flags Flying, American Patriotic Quilts as Expressions of Liberty*. New York: E.P. Dutton in Association with the Museum of American Folk Art, 1986.

Bishop, Robert, *American Folk Sculpture*. New York: E.P. Dutton, 1974.

Bishop, Robert, and Patricia Coblentz, *A Gallery of American Weathervanes and Whirligigs*. New York: E.P. Dutton, 1984.

Bishop, Robert, and Elizabeth Safanda, *A Gallery of Amish Quilts*. New York: E.P. Dutton & Co., Inc., 1976.

Charleston, Robert J., *World Ceramics*. London: Hamlyn, 1981.

Chaucer, Geoffrey, *The Canterbury Tales*, Nine Tales and the General Prologue with Authoritative Text Sources, selected and edited by V.A. Kolve and Glending Olson. New York: W.W. Norton & Company, 1989.

Chaucer, Geoffrey, *The Canterbury Tales*, translated by Nevill Coghill. New York: Penguin Books, 1977.

Chevalier, Jean and Alain Gheerbrant, *A Dictionary of Symbols*, translated by John Buchanan-Brown. New York: Penguin Books, 1996.

Cohen, J.M. and M. J. Cohen, *The New Penguin Dictionary of Quotations*. New York: Penguin Books, 1998.

Couderc, Philippe, *Les Plats Qui Ont Fait La France*. Paris: Editions Julliard, 1995.

Dinger, Charlotte, *Art of the Carousel*. Carousel Art, Inc., 1983.

Duke, Harvey, *Official Price Guide to Pottery and Porcelain*. 8th Ed. New York: House of Collectibles, 1995.

Eberhard, Wolfram, *A Dictionary of Chinese Symbols*. London: Routledge Press, 1998.

Ferguson, George, *Signs and Symbols in Christian Art*. New York & Cambridge: Oxford University Press, 1959.

Fontana, David, *The Secret Language of Symbols*. San Francisco: Chronicle Books, 1994.

Fraley, Tobin, *The Carousel Animal*. San Francisco: Chronicle Books, 1983.

Fraser, Antonia, *A History of Toys*. New York: Delacorte Press, 1966.

Herbst, Sharon Tyler, *Food Lover's Companion*, 2d Ed. Hauppauge: Barron's Educational Series, Inc., 1995.

Katz, Ephraim, *The Film Encyclopedia*. 3d Ed. New York: Harper Perennial, 1998.

Klamkin, Charles, *Weathervanes*, Hawthorn Books, 1973.

European Specialities. Vol. 1 and 2 of Culinaria. Chief Editors Römer, J., Ditter, M. Cologne: Konemann Verlagsgesellschaft gmbh, 1995

Kopp, Joel and Kate, *American Hooked and Sewn Rugs: Folk Art Underfoot*. New York: E.P. Dutton, Inc., 1985.

Lavitt, Wendy, *Animals in American Folk Art*. New York: Alfred A. Knopf, 1990.

Li, He, *Chinese Ceramics: A New Comprehensive Survey.* New York: Rizzoli International Publications, 1996.

Lowe, Warren, *Animals in Art.* Black Belt Press, 1997.

Meider, Wolfgang, Stewart A. Kingsbury, and Kelsie B. Harder, *A Dictionary of American Proverbs.* New York: Oxford University Press, 1992.

Mirror of the Medieval World. Edited by Wixom, W.D. New York: The Metropolitan Museum of Art, 1999.

Murray, Peter and Linda Murray, *The Oxford Companion to Christian Art and Architecture.* New York & Cambridge: Oxford University Press, 1996.

Newbound, Betty and Bill Newbound, *Collector's Encyclopedia of Milk Glass.* Paducah: Collector Books, 1995.

Pressland, David, *The Art of the Tin Toy.* New Cavendish Books, 1976.

Roberts, Allen F., *Animals in African Art: From the Familiar to the Marvelous.* Munich: The Museum for African Art, 1995.

Savage, George, *An Illustrated Dictionary of Ceramics.* London: Thames & Hudson, 1989.

Schoonmaker, Frank, *Encyclopedia of Wine.* London: Adam & Charles Black, 1979.

Selections from the Campbell Museum Collection. 5th Ed. Edited by Marion, John F. Camden: Campbell Museum, 1983.

Tannahill, Reay, *Food in History.* New York: Three Rivers Press, 1989.

The Knopf Collectors Guides to American Antiques, Folk Art, Paintings, Sculpture and Country Objects. New York: Alfred A. Knopf, 1982.

Toussaint-Samat, Maguelonne, *History of Food,* translated by Anthea Bell. Oxford & Malden: Blackwell Publishers, Inc., 1999.

Tresidder, Jack, *Dictionary of Symbols: An Illustrated Guide to Traditional Images, Icons, and Emblems.* San Francisco: Chronicle Books, 1998.

Twelve Centuries of Japanese Art from the Imperial Collections. Washington, D.C.: Freer Gallery of Art and the Arthur M. Sackler Gallery, in association with the Smithsonian Institute Press, 1997.

Vaughn, Mary Ann Woloch, *Ukrainian Easter.* Indiana: Ukrainian Heritage Co., 1983.

von Habsburg, Géza, *Fabergé in America.* London: Thames & Hudson, 1996.

Williams, C.A.S., *Chinese Symbolism and Art Motifs.* 3d Ed. Rev. Rutland: Charles E. Tuttle Co., 1991.

Sources

cover: Chicken ornament from the Flying Elephants, San Rafael, CA; *page i*: Rug courtesy of McAdoo Rugs, New York, NY; *pages ii and iii*: Author's collection, from Foutz Trading, Shiprock, NM.; *page v*: Tin lantern from author's collection, from Asian Antiques, Great Barrington, MA; *pages vi and vii*: Nesting hen from the collection of Richard Story and Jennifer Crandall; *page xi*: Brass rooster card holder from Bob Pryor Antiques, New York, NY. Rooster bookmark and wooden eggs from author's collection; *page xiii*: Selection of cards and notes and ceramic chickens from author's collection; *page xiv*: Tray from La Terrine, New York, NY. Staffordshire nesting hen from Bob Pryor Antiques, New York, NY. Statuette from the collection of Carole Lalli; *page xv and xvi*: Photograph of Greek urn courtesy of The Bridgeman Art Library, used by permission; *page xvii*: Photograph of fresco from the Museo Nazionale di Capodimonte, Naples, Italy, courtesy of Art Resource, used by permission; *page 1*: Wedgewood platter from author's collection; *page 4*: Photograph of painting from

The Bridgeman Art Library, © 2000 Artists Rights Society (ARS), New York, ADAGP, Paris; *page 6*: Coffee mugs from author's collection; *pages 8 and 10*: Porcelain rooster from the author's collection, from Sur La Table, Seattle, WA. Tablecloth and napkins from the Horchow Home Collection (Irving, TX); *page 13*: Nineteenth-century rooster shop sign and chicken basket from Country Loft Antiques, Woodbury, CT. 1920s lawn ornament courtesy of Ron and Priscilla Richley. All others from author's collection; *page 15*: Toile scenic tablecloth made from printed fabric "Ile de France, Houdan" available from Pierre Deux Fabrics, New York, NY. Rooster tea towel by Kitchen Crate, Kay Dee Designs, Hope Valley, RI, all from author's collection; *pages 16 and 17*: Red rooster printed cloth from Stroheim and Romann, Inc., New York, NY. Rooster and hen cushion courtesy of Gracious Home, New York, NY; *page 18*: Hen plate from author's collection, available from Alison Palmer Studio, Pawling, NY; *page 19*: Painting by Melinda K. Hall. The artist's work is availabe from Patri-

cia Carlisle Fine Art Inc., Santa Fe, NM; *page 20*: The author's chicken teapot by CBK Ltd. is available from Chatelaine, New York, NY; *page 21*: Postcard courtesy of a private collector. *page 22*: *Chicken Little* book from author's collection, is a 1958 edition published by Western Publishing Co. Inc. of Racine, WI; *page 23*: Glass nesting hen from author's collection; Staffordshire hen from the collection of Ron and Priscilla Richley; *page 25*: All kitchen items from author's collection. Clay pot by Rompertoff, pottery jar reproduced by the Boscobel Restoration, Garrison, NY and clay bread warmer by Boston Warehouse; *page 26*: (On the table) hen candlesticks and chicken couple figurines from author's collection; hen pedestal cranberry glass courtesy of Sue Blair. Napkins and tablecloth made from "Home to Roost" print by the Cranston Collections, Cranston, RI. (On the mantle) china hen and rooster courtesy of Gracious Home, New York, NY; *page 29*: Rooster bank from author's collection; *page 31*: Platter from author's collection; *pages 32 and 33*: Fighting cocks tray from author's collection; cocktail napkins and tea towel (opposite) courtesy of Sue Blair. Colorful statues courtesy of Joel Siegel and April 56, Lakeville, CT; *page 34:* Rooster chef statue courtesy of Bob Rush and available from Church Street Trading Company, Great Barrington, MA; *page 38:* Nesting hen courtesy of Ilene Bahr; *page 40:* Ceramic platter from author's collection, available from La Terrine, New York, NY; *pages 42 and 43:* Jug, creamer, and salt and pepper shakers from author's collection. *pages 44 and 45:* Brass statuettes and dinner bell on table are from Bob Pryor Antiques, New York, NY. Pathé Freres brass figure is from the collection of Sue Blair; *page 46:* Ceramic rooster statue, from author's collection, is available from Belle Maison, Newton, MA; *page 47:* Crowing cock clock from Bob Pryor Antiques, New York, NY; *page 48:* nineteenth-century sign from Bob Pryor Antiques, New York, NY; *page 49:* Greeting card from a private collection; *pages 50 and 51:* Baby chick dishes are courtesy of Sue Blair; rooster plates and table linens from author's collection and available from Panache, Matteson, IL. Drinking glasses are available from Pan American Phoenix, New York, NY; *page 52:* All chicken objects courtesy of Olde

Antiques Market, Great Barrington, MA; *page 53:* Chicken print from author's collection; "putz" courtesy of Ron and Priscilla Richley; *page 55:* Rooster lamp courtesy of Sue Blair, needlework cushion by Joseph Mann and the glass, coaster, and cloth are from the author's collection; *page 56:* Photograph of rug courtesy of "America Hurrah Archives, N.Y.C."; *page 57:* Silhouette for flag pole courtesy of Coffman's Antique Markets, Great Barrington, MA; *page 58:* Postcard from private collection; *page 59:* Border printed cloth from "Home to Roost" print in author's collection by the Cranston Collections, Cranston, RI; *pages 60 and 61:* Glasses and napkin rings from author's collection. All other chicken figures courtesy of Ron and Priscilla Richley; *pages 62 and 63:* Milk glass nesting hen and chick courtesy of Olde Antiques, Great Barrington, MA; *page 63:* Metal door and drawer knobs courtesy of Gracious Home, New York, NY; *pages 63 and 64:* Chicken-topped skewers from the collection of Carole Lalli; *page 66:* Rooster bowl courtesy of April 56, Lakeville, CT; *page 67:* Pair of Chinese rooster statuettes courtesy of Renato Danese; *page 68:* Seed chicken from author's collection. Mexican tin lanterns and

glassware from Pan American Phoenix, New York, NY. Rooster needlepoint cushion in background by Roz Music. Orange ceramic chargers from La Terrine, New York, NY. Table runner available from Twining Weavers, Taos, NM; *page 69:* Hen planter courtesy of a private collector. *page 72:* Porcelain hen from the collection of Carole Lalli; engraving courtesy of Country Loft Antiques, Woodbury, CT. Photographed at the Sheepherding Company of Old Chatham, NY; *pages 74 and 75:* Iron doorstops from author's collection, available from Upper Deck Ltd., New Bedford, MA; *page 77:* Chicken plates (available from the Horchow Home Collection, Irving, TX) and nickknacks from the collection of Carole Lalli. Printed fabric from Stroheim and Romann, Inc., New York, NY; *page 79:* Wooden mold from the collection of Sue Blair; *page 80:* Author's collection of kitchen towels; *page 81:* Plate from breakfast service in author's collection; *pages 82 and 83:* Antique egg dish and oil jug from the collection of Carole Lalli; *pages 84 and 85:* Pottery hen from Country Loft Antiques of Woodbury, CT. Drawing of hen from author's collection. Raffia hen from April 56 of Lakeville, CT; *page 86:* Bottle stopper from author's collection; *pages 88 and 89:* Hanging tin silhouette and chicken motif glasses from April 56, Lakeville, CT. Taxidermy chicken courtesy of William Hicks and William Sadler. From the author's collection are the wood carved and painted chickens on the table, in the basket, and at the far right on the bench as well as the twig and stick chickens, the latter available from Wildwood International of Omaha, Nebraska, and the printed napkin at lower left. The rooster assembled from a craft kit is courtesy of Fernando Music. The garden rooster, pottery bowl, and salad servers are courtesy of Carole Lalli; *pages 90 and 91:* Wood carving by Kaminski and paper cut out from Folk Arts of Poland, Santa Fe, NM; *page 93:* Mola from author's collection. Plate courtesy of Joel Siegel; *pages 94 and 95:* Jade statuette from the collection of Sheila Klodney. Rooster neck piece from author's collection, available at Asian Arts, Great Barrington, MA. Ceramic chopstick holders from author's collection; *page 96:* Rooster figure from artist Bob Johnson, Santa Fe, NM; *page 97:* Biscuit tins from Country Loft Antiques, Woodbury, CT; *page 100:* Chicken coop photograph from Corbis-Bettman; *pages 102 and 103:* Glazed hen

and painted wooden hen are from the author's collection (Edith John's work is available from Foutz Trading, Shiprock, NM); *page 105:* Rooster and hen platter courtesy of The Emporium, Great Barrington, MA; *page 107:* Tureen courtesy of Winterthur Museum; *page 108:* Tall goblet from April 56, Lakeville, CT. Juice glass at far right from author's collection. Wine glass, tumbler, and cranberry glass courtesy of Sue Blair; *page 109:* Drinking jar from author's collection; *page 111:* Plate courtesy of Carole Lalli; *pages 112 and 113:* Brass statuettes courtesy of Sue Blair. Faux stone rooster from April 56, Lakeville, CT; *pages 114 and 115:* Tureen and plate are available from La Terrine, New York, NY; *page 117:* Large metal mold from Bob Pryor Antiques, New York, NY; small mold courtesy of Sue Blair. Table linens and the napkin ring (available at La Terrine, New York NY) are from the author's collection; *page 118:* Antique print from the author's collection; *page 119:* Author's pin from Dorothy Bauer, Berkley, CA; *pages 120 and 121:* Antique print on far left and fourth from left from the collection of Joseph Mann. Print on far right courtesy of Country Loft Antiques, Woodbury, CT. All others from author's collection. Pho-

tographed at the Sheepherding Company of Old Chatham, NY; *page 123:* Plate (available from Peggy Ganstad, Santa Fe, NM), salt and pepper shakers, and planter are all from the author's collection; *page 124:* Pecking hen and fighting cock toys on trunk top and tin egg laying hen on floor are from author's collection. Pecking toy on trunk at right from the collection of Ron and Priscilla Richley. Pull toys on floor at left and right courtesy of Country Loft Antiques, Woodbury, CT; *page 125:* Pull toy courtesy of Ron and Priscilla Richley; *pages 126 and 127:* From author's collection: hanging ornaments of bristles or in wood, kitchen timer by Bon Jour, wooden hen with drawer, printed boxes by Poppyprint, spreaders from Williams Sonoma, paper napkins by Caspari, napkin holder, and antique potholder. Antique jam pot courtesy of Ilene Bahr. Hen bowl at far left and jugs at center and right are courtesy of Carole Lalli. Kitchen plaque is from La Terrine, New York, NY. Scrapbook rooster is courtesy of Ron and Priscilla Richley. Antique print is from Country Loft Antiques, Woodbury, CT; *page 128:* Rug runner by McAdoo, New York, NY; *page 129:* Rooster decorative plaque from La Terrine, NY; *page 131:* Blue glass objects from author's collection; *pages 132 and 133:* Kitchen tiles available from Quimper Faience, Stonington, CT; *page 135:* Plates available from Quimper Faience, Stonington, CT; *page 138:* Quilt courtesy of artist Nancy Halpern; *page 140:* Weathervane from the archives of Art Resource; *page 141:* Weathervane courtesy of Country Loft Antiques, Woodbury, CT; *pages 142 and 143:* Fabergé eggs from the Forbes Magazine Collection, NY; *pages 144 and 145:* Decorative eggs from the collection of Ron and Priscilla Richley; *page 146:* Serving bowl courtesy of the artist, Ron Meyers. *page 147:* Ceramic cannister is

Royal Rooster by Village Pottery, courtesy of Gracious Home. Chicken border bowls and plates from La Terrine, New York, NY and the collection of Joe Siegel. Chicken potholder by Stevens Linens and napkin are from the author's collection; *page 148:* Photograph of carved totem from the Newark Museum, Walter Dormitzer Collection, provided by the archives of Art Resource; *pages 150 and 151:* Collection of tea towels from Sue Blair; *page 152:* Card from a private collection; *page 153:* Paper, painted, and carved decorative eggs, chicken toys and candy dispenser from author's collection; *page 154:* Tea cozy

from Coffman Antiques, Great Barrington, MA. Tea cup courtesy of Carole Lalli. Tea towel by Kai-Dee Designs from author's collection; *page 155:* Photograph of carousel rooster provided by Tobin Fraley and Chronicle Books, San Francisco; *page 157:* Statue and shakers from author's collection. Deviled egg dish from the collection of Carole Lalli. Painting courtesy of Ron and Priscilla Richley; *page 158:* Painting from the outsider art collection of Robert Hicks; *page 159:* Wire basket courtesy of Maggie Rodford; *pages 160 and 161:* Egg cups selected from the collections of Carole Lalli and Ron and Priscilla Richley.

Metric Conversion Charts

The metric weights given in this chart are not exact equivalents, but have been rounded up or down slightly to make measuring easier.

Avoirdupois	Metric
¼ oz	7 g
½ oz	15 g
1 oz	30 g
2 oz	60 g
3 oz	90 g
4 oz	115 g
5 oz	150 g
6 oz	175 g
7 oz	200 g
8 oz (½ lb)	225 g
9 oz	250 g
10 oz	300 g
11 oz	325 g
12 oz	350 g
13 oz	375 g
14 oz	400 g
15 oz	425 g
16 oz (1 lb)	450 g
1½ lb	750 g
2 lb	900 g
2¼ lb	1 kg
3 lb	1.4 kg
4 lb	1.8 kg

VOLUME EQUIVALENTS

These are not exact equivalents for American cups and spoons, but have been rounded up or down slightly to make measuring easier.

American	Metric	Imperial
¼ t	1.2 ml	
½ t	2.5 ml	
1 t	5.0 ml	
½ T (1.5 t)	7.5 ml	
1 T (3 t)	15 ml	
¼ cup (4 T)	60 ml	2 fl oz
⅓ cup (5 T)	75 ml	2 1ff2 fl oz
½ cup (8 T)	125 ml	4 fl oz
⅔ cup (10 T)	150 ml	5 fl oz
¾ cup (12 T)	175 ml	6 fl oz
1 cup (16 T)	250 ml	8 fl oz
1¼ cups	300 ml	10 fl oz (½ pt)
1½ cups	350 ml	12 fl oz
2 cups (1 pint)	500 ml	16 fl oz
2½ cups	625 ml	20 fl oz (1 pint)
1 quart	1 liter	32 fl oz

OVEN TEMPERATURE EQUIVALENTS

Oven Mark	F	C	Gas
Very cool	250-275	130-140	½–1
Cool	300	150	2
Warm	325	170	3
Moderate	350	180	4
Moderately hot	375	190	5
	400	200	6
Hot	425	220	7
	450	230	8
Very hot	475	250	9

INDEX